Impact

Impact

How Assistant Principals Can Be High Performing Leaders

Christopher Colwell

ROWMAN & LITTLEFIELD
Lanham • Boulder • New York • London

Published by Rowman & Littlefield
A wholly owned subsidiary of The Rowman & Littlefield Publishing Group, Inc.
4501 Forbes Boulevard, Suite 200, Lanham, Maryland 20706
www.rowman.com

Unit A, Whitacre Mews, 26-34 Stannary Street, London SE11 4AB

British Library Cataloguing in Publication Information Available

Library of Congress Cataloging-in-Publication Data

Colwell, Christopher.
How assistant principals can be high performing leaders / Christopher Colwell.
pages cm.
Includes bibliographical references.
ISBN 978-1-4758-1105-6 (cloth : alk. paper) — ISBN 978-1-4758-1106-3 (pbk. : alk. paper) —
ISBN 978-1-4758-1107-0 (electronic)
1. Assistant school principals—United States. 2. School management and organization—United
States. 3. Educational leadership—United States. I. Title.
LB2831.92.C64 2015
371.200973—dc23

2015000500

∞™ The paper used in this publication meets the minimum requirements of American
National Standard for Information Sciences Permanence of Paper for Printed Library
Materials, ANSI/NISO Z39.48-1992.

Printed in the United States of America

Contents

Foreword

It was, as they say, "back in the day" when I first met Chris Colwell. By luck of the scheduling draw we were enrolled in the same class at the outset of our doctoral studies and had a mutual friend who introduced us as we sat pensively waiting for the professor to enter the room. To be perfectly candid, I did not make an instant connection with the guy when he parked himself across the table from me. I attributed my initial impressions to the fact that he was an elementary school assistant principal and I was a high school assistant principal. Both of us were early into our careers as school administrators, and I assumed that because we were living in different worlds we just had different perspectives.

What I quickly came to learn was my first impression completely missed the mark. He is one of the most cerebral yet practical educators I have ever known. That is a curious combination, but if you knew Chris, you would know exactly what I mean. He has this uncanny knack for being able to sift through the most complicated issues to distill them into understandable parts and then generate pragmatic solutions to those issues.

Just having those skills is enough to separate the average school administrator from the exceptional school administrator. However, what really distinguishes Chris from other school administrators, which I have known over my forty-one years in the profession, is his ability to clearly communicate potential solutions to challenging issues at all levels of the organization.

Simply put, Chris "gets it." He has done it again with the writing of *Impact: How Assistant Principals Can Be High Performing Leaders*. Utilizing relevant research and drawing from his personal experience made over the course of his notable career as a teacher, guidance counselor, assistant principal, elementary school principal, middle school principal, high school principal, assistant superintendent, deputy superintendent, and university professor he has captured the essence of the evolving role of the assistant principal in the schools of today and those of tomorrow.

High performing schools require high performing leaders. In the first chapter, the context and forces leading to the realization that leadership in schools can no longer be thought to reside only in the office of the principal is established. What follows in the subsequent chapters is a clear explanation of the key roles the assistant principal can and should play in building a collegial and collaborative culture of shared leadership in a school. It is here where the real payoff of this text resides. Real-world examples of the challenges assistant principals face are coupled with concrete recommendations for avoiding career derailers and building credibility as a leadership partner with the principal, faculty, and staff of the school, parents, community members, and district leaders.

The need for a resource like this is long overdue. Those aspiring to become school administrators should not have to guess what the role of the assistant principal truly involves. They also need the opportunity to learn from the experiences of others, like those shared in this book, so they are better prepared to transition into the role on their appointment as an assistant principal.

Impact: How Assistant Principals Can Be High Performing Leaders does not just provide a road map to those who aspire to become assistant principals. It provides a flight plan they can refer to throughout their career to further develop and refine their leadership skills. The insights gained in each chapter promote continuous professional growth. These insights also provide readers the opportunity to develop problem solving skills that can contribute to them becoming highly effective professional educators prepared to make significant contributions to the success of the overall operation of a school.

Current assistant principals who seek to engage in transformative leadership have even more to gain from reading, studying and applying the strategies contained in the book because they are actively immersed in the role. Without equivocation, I am convinced that the insights shared can assist any assistant principal, at any grade level, in becoming a high performing/high contributing member on their school's leadership team.

It has been said that if you can't explain it simply, you don't understand it well enough. Well, after reading *Impact: How Assistant Principals Can Be High Performing Leaders,* you'll know that Chris Colwell understands the many challenges and issues that confront assistant principals today. You'll also appreciate the easy-to-read format and common-sense strategies that he has provided to support the professional growth and leadership development of assistant principals over the span of their careers.

Ron Pinnell, EdD
Director of Leadership Pathways
Seminole County Public Schools
Seminole County, Florida

Preface

Much has been written about the role of the principal as an instructional leader. Research suggests that the quality of the principal is second only to the quality of the classroom teacher when it comes to impacting student achievement. Far too little attention, however, has been paid to the pivotal role that assistant principals have in the development of high performing schools. *Impact: How Assistant Principals Can Be High Performing Leaders,* provides specific, practical, and replicable leadership strategies that great assistant principals use to make a difference in their schools and their communities.

Part I ("The Principal Partner") examines the challenges and opportunities assistant principals experience with the school principal. Opportunities and strategies for building a unique principal–assistant principal partnership are considered. *Impact* describes how to manage the inevitable change of the school principal; how to build meaningful principal–assistant principal leadership teams; and how to "lead up" so that the principal, district staff, and superintendent see the assistant principal as a leader of leaders. The attributes and behaviors that a principal needs and looks for in the assistant principal partner are also examined.

Part II ("The Faculty Partner") examines the challenges faced by assistant principals, as well as the opportunities to serve as an instructional leader and partner with the school faculty. This section focuses on the specific opportunities assistant principals have to be the instructional leader of the school and to be the voice of the faculty, as well as the principal, by leveraging the unique opportunities for leadership that are only available to the assistant principal—in other words, how to "lead from the middle."

Part III ("The Assistant Principal as Instructional Leader") looks at the assistant principal as an instructional leader in the middle of the organization, working between the principal and the faculty. *Impact* examines the art and science of the assistant principal as a school leader, as a leader who makes a difference in the lives of teachers and students in significant ways. An examination of how it is that some assistant principals achieve significance far beyond their job title and of the behaviors, attributes, and skill sets high performing assistant principals use with great effect is conducted. This section examines the unique challenges and opportunities presented to the assistant principal that are distinct from the position of the principal or classroom teacher.

Finally, Part IV ("The Assistant Principal and Daily Operations") examines the challenges, and strategies for overcoming those challenges, caused by the often overwhelming number of management tasks typically assigned to the assistant principal. An examination of the effective management of student conduct, of student and faculty rights in the workplace, and of effective family and community partnerships is included in this section.

Impact is a practitioner's guide for the assistant principal striving to be a true school leader. Target audiences include teachers wishing to become assistant principals; current assistant principals looking to excel and lead careers of significance from the platform of the assistant principalship; colleges of education working with graduate students who are being trained to enter the field of P–12 school administration; and sitting school principals looking to understand, and benefit from, the often underutilized, potential of the assistant principal to lead schools.

Great assistant principals matter. They are critical to the overall "instructional health" of the school and the overall ability of both the principal and the faculty to accomplish their jobs. *Impact: How Assistant Principals Can Be High Performing Leaders* has been written to assist and support all assistant principals, as well as the principals, teachers, and stakeholders who work each and every day to make a difference in the lives of children.

Acknowledgments

For thirty-seven years I have had the pleasure of working with, and supporting, outstanding assistant principals, teachers, school principals, and university professors who work tirelessly to impact the lives of students. To all of those educators who have afforded me the honor of being their colleague, I am deeply grateful.

To all the assistant principals and principals who have informed my practice and thinking on the nature of the assistant principal, I say thank you. To Judy Winch, Andrea Schwamb, Caroline Zendt, Shannon Hay, Chris Pryor, and Carol Kelly, thank you for your reflections on the nature of school leadership and the assistant principal. To all of my colleagues in the education department at Stetson University, to Milba Miranda and Dean Karen Ryan, who afforded me the opportunity to participate in their scholarly activities and have provided me with assistance on this project whenever needed, a special thank you. To Jane Bradford, who provided expert editorial support, thank you.

Thanks to Glen Epley who provided significant guidance and input in the areas of school law and the role of the assistant principal, to Rajni Shankar-Brown for her insights into the role of school leaders in the middle school setting, and to Ron Pinnell and Andrea Schwamb for their review of the manuscript and insights into the nature of the twenty-first-century school leader.

Lastly, to my mother, Ann Colwell, and my wife, Monique, thank you for all your love, support, feedback, and patience throughout this entire project.

I

The Principal Partner

ONE

Building a Principal–Assistant Principal Partnership Team

Look at any job description or read any article regarding the role of the principal in the school, and you will inevitably see the term *instructional leader*. The principal is the instructional leader of the school. It is the principal who is tasked with the ultimate responsibility for teaching and learning within the school setting, of establishing the conditions that result in quality instruction for all students (Hallinger & Walker, 2010). It is the principal who is charged with establishing the culture and vision of the school and the climate in which the school will operate (Zepeda, 2013). It is often said that behind every high performing school, there is a high performing principal. How the principal interacts with the faculty in the school sets the tone, culture, and climate of the school. "Of all the relationships that exist within a school, none has a greater effect on the quality of life than the relationship between the teacher and the principal" (Green, 2013, p. 119). In today's complex school environment, where the principal cannot succeed in isolation, the relationship between the assistant principal and the principal, as well as the relationship between the assistant principal and the faculty, has great impact on the quality of life and work within the school.

SCHOOL LEADERSHIP AS A COLLECTIVE PROCESS

Look at any analysis of leadership in today's school setting. There is an overwhelming consensus regarding the increasing complexity of the school organization itself, as well as the goals and expectations the principal is expected to meet. Just as with our society as a whole, schools today operate in an age of ever-accelerating change in an era of globalization

(Bess & Goldman, 2001). Today's schools are expected to prepare graduates who can compete for jobs in a world economy where there is increased competition for talent and increased opportunities for companies to headquarter anywhere there is cheap, reliable, and skilled labor.

For school leaders in the twenty-first-century schools will not only operate in much more complex climates than in previous decades but will also be subjected to ever-increasing competition from the private sector, from charter schools, school vouchers, other forms of school choice, online schools, and other uses of technology as an alternative to the schoolhouse as the best or only place to access an education. One result of all of this complexity and competition is a call for collaborative leadership by the principal, for leadership strategies and techniques designed to facilitate and support the work of teachers and other stakeholders through the use of expert power rather than position power (Gruenert, 2005). Modern leadership is seen—not just in the education sector but in the private sector as well—as a collective process (Drath, 2001; Raelin, 2003).

An emerging trend in the private sector is to shift the emphasis from the development of individual "leaders" as the main goal of leadership development to developing skills among teams of leaders and followers. If effective leadership is seen as a social process that engages everyone in the organization, then it doesn't make sense to invest exclusively in the skills of one individual leader. Developing the capacity for a "system for leadership" is at least as important as developing the capacity of individual leaders (Hubbard, 2005).

Many private sector companies are finding that the individually oriented model of the leader is limited in its capacity to cope with the challenging conditions that are becoming typical in today's society. The army has developed an acronym for the modern environment in which organizations and leaders operate: VUCA—volatile, uncertain, complex, and ambiguous (Hesselbein & Shinseki, 2004). Most educators and educational leaders would agree that today's schools operate in volatile, uncertain, complex, and ambiguous climates. Leaders of complex organizations, which public education certainly is, are going to need collective thinking to solve many of the problems faced today. Bringing about organizational change will require more than any single leader can achieve on their own. Team-based approaches are not only much more likely to be successful; they also help avoid burnout of senior leaders by building support throughout the organization. In addition, teams of leaders can support one another when they find themselves dealing with cultures within the organization that are not supportive of the organization's mission.

Today's modern schools are complex and dynamic, open social systems. Today's modern schools face all the complexities and challenges faced by any large organization. There is a wide variety of internal and external stakeholders impacting the culture, climate, and morale of the students and adults in the building. It is simply not reasonable to expect one leader, the principal, to impact the complex social systems that exist within schools. The principal must be more than the instructional leader of the school; the principal must be a leader of an instructional leadership team, a leader of a community of learners. No high performing principal leads alone. Leadership is a collective process. Leadership is a team sport, and the assistant principal can and should play a major role in how teaching and learning occur in the school, as well as nurture the culture and climate of the school. Perhaps it is more accurate to say that a core component in every high performing school is more than a high performing principal: it is a high performing leadership team.

SCHOOL LEADERSHIP AS THE DEVELOPMENT OF PERSONAL QUALITIES

There has also been an emphasis in the literature for some time regarding the need to develop the personal qualities of leaders, the recognition that leading is personal, that most leaders develop through formal learning and experiences (Day & Halpin, 2001). Incorporating personal development as an element of effective leadership is becoming a key component of private sector and military sector leadership training (Burns, 1978). All sectors of our society are also witness to a series of reminders regarding the importance of ethics in leadership and the impact that unethical and fraudulent leadership behavior can have on organizations, from Lehman Brothers and Citibank to the standardized assessment scandal that rocked the Fulton County, Georgia, School District (Senge, Smith, Kruschwitz, Laur, & Schley, 2008). Most scholars now assume that while some leaders may be "born" (i.e., possess traits that were either inherited or acquired at an early age), most are "made" (i.e., learn much of their ability to lead from experience and formal learning). Leaders are made, not born; leadership skills can be developed (Benne, 1948; Kippenberger, 1997; Day & Halpin, 2001; Ruvolo, Peterson, & LeBouf, 2004). The assistant principal can and should be considered key as a leader within the school leadership team. The assistant principal should actively participate in the collective process of the school, be a key figure in both the receiving and dispensing of personal leadership skill training in key leadership attributes such as interpersonal skills, facilitation skills, and assessment and feedback skills.

An important dimension of leading is the ability to cultivate leadership skills in subordinates who have it naturally. It is also important to cultivate the development of leadership skills in those not necessarily born leaders. In other words, training, coaching, mentoring, and assessing current and future leaders matters. All of the issues facing today's schools and the recommendations being made regarding how effective leaders should function provide wonderful opportunities for the assistant principal who wishes to impact the school in significant ways to do just that—impact teaching and learning as an instructional leader.

BUILDING THE PRINCIPAL–ASSISTANT PRINCIPAL TEAM

Today's principal cannot be successful without high performing assistant principals who bring expertise and passion to the job, who are leaders in their own right. An important point for the assistant principal and the principal to recognize is that it is in the principal's best interest to have a high performing, productive, problem solving assistant principal as a leadership colleague. A well-regarded and successful high school principal shared with the author this comment regarding the need for assistant principals to be engaged in the work and active with input and problem solving suggestions. The principal said, "I know what I think; I want to know what the assistant principal thinks." The era of the principal as the sole leader of the school who operates independently and in isolation from all stakeholders is over. The era of the assistant principal as just an administrative manager or member of the principal's support staff is over.

When the principal–assistant principal relationship is built around trust, loyalty, a common mission, and a common philosophy, the ability of the principal to accomplish the task of building a school community of learners where teachers can reach their potential and students thrive emotionally, socially, and academically is greatly enhanced. When the principal–assistant principal relationship lacks these essential elements, the value of the assistant principal is greatly diminished.

KEYS TO BUILDING A HIGH PERFORMING PRINCIPAL–ASSISTANT PRINCIPAL LEADERSHIP TEAM

There are many opportunities and pitfalls to both the development and maintenance a productive principal–assistant principal team. Understanding what an instructional partnership is, and what it is not, is fundamental to building trust within the administrative team. Highly effective leadership teams understand the power of the team as opposed to the power of any one individual within the team. Understanding the "power of we" is an important prerequisite for effective team building. The ability to communicate effectively and consistently is another powerful prerequisite for effective partnerships between the principal and the assistant principal, as well as between the assistant principal and other school stakeholders (Baldoni, 2004; Gilley, Gilley, & McMillan, 2009). Finally, while it may not be intuitive, the power of mistakes, of how mistakes are handled by the leadership team, will provide many opportunities to build team cohesion and effectiveness.

The Power of "We"

It does take a team to lead a school. It takes talented teachers, involved parents, school administrators who are instructional leaders, dedicated support staff and district support, and countless other stakeholders both within and outside the formal organization known as a school. The assistant principal is part of a leadership team. It is within that structure of the team that the assistant principals can and should develop and use their expert power and their charismatic power in order to be an instructional leader. It is the power of "we," not the power of the position or the individual, that will provide the greatest opportunity to impact teaching and learning. When it comes to building a positive and effective principal–assistant principal leadership team, assistant principals should begin by removing the word "I" from their vocabulary. When addressing the faculty, parents, or any other stakeholders, high performing assistant principals discuss what the team has done, what "we" are accomplishing and doing for students, not what they, as individuals have done. Certainly there will be any number of meetings with the principal, faculty, or stakeholders when individual opinions, including the opinions of the assistant principal, are sought out and should be shared. The outcomes of those meetings, however the solutions are rendered or the action plans developed, are the work of a team, not an individual. When the assistant principal operates primarily from a team orientation rather than an individual orientation, trust and respect from both the faculty and the principal will follow.

The Power of Communication

Much has been written about the power of communication, and correctly so. How leaders communicate—verbally, nonverbally, and with written communication—will determine to a great extent how effective the leaders will be. How leaders communicate says a great deal about how leaders perceive and use power. The types and tone of communication from autocratic leaders who rely on position power will be very different from the styles and tone of leaders who rely on expert and collegial power. The power of communication exists whether the platform is a large group such as a faculty, student body, or group of parents, or if the platform is very small and consists of just two individuals. How the assistant principal and the principal communicate with each other behind closed doors and how the assistant principal and the principal communicate with other stakeholders in public settings will establish the tone and effectiveness of the leadership team itself.

These patterns, tones, and uses of communication impact the quality of the team's work, whether the communication is part of a formal process or is part of the myriad of informal communications that occur every day. The establishment of a formal structure for communicating as a leadership team is recommended. Since effective and productive communication is a key to an effective and productive leadership team, a formal structure and calendar for leadership team meetings is necessary. Effective principals and assistant principals work to assure that ongoing scheduled opportunities to meet and discuss management and leadership issues impacting the school are occurring. These meetings may be scheduled on a weekly basis in which an agenda for discussing and collaborating on significant issues and school goals can be discussed in depth. Other models include a daily fifteen-minute minimeeting during which the team meets briefly to review the day's goals and activities and to provide brief updates regarding any time-sensitive issues. Establishing expectations for how communication with all stakeholders will occur and how the leadership team will keep itself up to speed with all the informal meetings and discussions that take place each day is also a critical component of the communication system between the principal and the assistant principal. When a system for allowing communication is in place and a set of expectations for how and when open communication will occur is in place, the leadership team will be able to harness the power of effective communication, as opposed to falling victim to the pitfalls of poor, inconsistent, or disjointed communication. In short, the principal and assistant principal are either communicating as a team, or the absence of communication indicates that they are not a team.

THE POWER OF MISTAKES

Educators don't often think of mistakes as opportunities. Unfortunately, in many ways our current education model has made making a mistake the worst thing that can happen in a school setting (Robinson, 2010). Students are taught that there is one correct answer to every problem. Teachers are taught that there is one set of best practices for instruction and assessment. Administrators are taught there is one set of policies, procedures, and practices to follow. In fact, mistakes are the building blocks for creativity and progress. It is what one does with the mistake, how one responds to the mistake, that makes the difference. Every mistake an assistant principal might make is an opportunity to learn and grow. Every mistake is an opportunity to be coached by the principal or by faculty leaders.

When the assistant principal makes a mistake in a public venue, it is important that the correction of that mistake also be made by the assistant principal. Certainly the assistant principal and principal should meet in order to understand the issues at hand and the underlying assumptions that resulted in the error and to then map out a plan to remedy the mistake. This is a powerful coaching opportunity that can be very effective in building the sense of team and of trust between the principal and the assistant principal. The correction of the error and, most importantly, the individual who publicly corrects the error should be the assistant principal. Providing a platform for the assistant principal to correct a public error with a public solution allows the assistant principal to maintain a leadership perspective with the faculty or the stakeholders involved in the issue at hand. This also prevents faculty and other stakeholders from wanting to go over the assistant principal's head directly to the principal for resolution of issues that can and should be managed at the assistant principal level. This approach to publicly correcting the errors or omissions that have been made publicly is the same approach the principal needs from district administrators when there is an error out of the principal's office. Just as no principal would want to be publicly overridden and corrected by their superiors, the assistant principal needs the same protection and opportunity to be the face and the voice that gets to correct the inevitable mistakes that will surely occur.

PRINCIPAL–ASSISTANT PRINCIPAL RELATIONSHIP TRAPS

There are also several common relationship traps that the school principal and assistant principal can fall into. These can be avoided by understanding what the traps are and how to navigate around them. Avoiding relationship traps such as "the loyalty trap," "the good cop–bad cop trap," and "the manager-leader trap" is critical to the success and positive impact of the team. Understanding the team behaviors that inhibit faculty trust and support of the principal and the assistant principal and understanding how to avoid those behaviors will help establish leadership that facilitates teaching and learning within the school.

The Loyalty Trap

Interviews with principals regarding the attributes they look for and need in a successful assistant principal partner often include adjectives such as hard working, mission driven, goal oriented, proactive, smart, and loyal. Of these descriptors, loyalty often comes first. One highly regarded principal with a reputation for mentoring assistant principals over a period of years said, "A successful assistant principal must be loyal to the principal. The faculty must see the principal and the assistant principal as a leadership team with a common mission." Another principal said, "Communication is the key to a successful principal–assistant principal relationship. Both parties must work for what is best for the school and the team. You have to be a servant to the team. The principal and the assistant principal have to have each other's backs. It is lonely up here." Loyalty and having the principal's back, however, do not mean the assistant principal should be a yes-man without an opinion on any initiative or plan of action. Being unwilling to present a point of view that is different from the principal's current thinking or being silent when an alternate pathway or process should be considered is not loyalty to the principal; it is a type of dereliction of duty. The principal has a right to know all the information t available that might impact the success of a decision or course of action. The principal should expect that any member of the leadership team will intervene with a suggested alternative course of action should the principal's decision or plan of action appear to be in violation of any school, district, state, or federal policy. In fact, the more the assistant principal knows about a subject or course of action and is skilled at understanding the formal and informal communication networks at play in the school and how the actions of the principal will be perceived and interpreted, the more valuable the assistant principal becomes. That value is only realized, however, if the assistant principal speaks up!

High performing leaders recognize that complex problems often require complex solutions. Complex solutions require brainstorming, quality decision making, two-way communication, critical thinking, and a thorough vetting of multiple strategies and outcomes associated with those strategies. The high performing principal cannot and does not want to plan and decide in isolation. The high performing principal wants an assistant principal who is a critical thinker, who is knowledgeable about the issues at hand, who understands the climate of the school, and most importantly can articulate alternate courses of action and provide rationale for recommendations made. What the principal wants, however, is for those discussions to occur in settings that are designed for open dialogue and discussion. A twenty-year high school principal with a reputation throughout her district for identifying and mentoring assistant principals described this ability to be both loyal and proactive this way: "Can the principal and the assistant principal argue for an hour behind closed doors about how to proceed in any given situation? Can they defend their positions and commit to their point of view, but do so in a way that demonstrates good communication skills and interpersonal relationships and, most importantly, once a final decision is reached, have unanimity in purpose, commitment, and support for the final decision?" A frank exchange of ideas and disagreements over alternative courses of action can occur in private meetings, but by no means should this type of discussion be limited to closed-doors meetings only. There are any number of important public settings with faculty, students, and other stakeholders, where quality decision making will only occur when there is a free exchange of ideas in a climate of trust and respect. What the common denominator needs to be for all of these venues for problem solving and a frank and professional exchange of ideas is the understanding from the principal that the forum in question is designed for that purpose. Just as the principal is expected to advise superiors regarding district office decisions while at the same time carrying out the final plan of action with fidelity and public support, so too does the principal want the best thinking of the assistant principal at all times, especially when that thinking would support alternative solutions. What the principal expects, what is meant by the term "loyalty" in the dynamic relationship between the principal and the assistant principal, is the ability of the assistant principal to also support the principal in the public implementation of decisions made.

The ability to impact the quality and appropriateness of decisions made by superiors is a common skill for high performing principals and assistant principals (Huffman, Hipp, Pankake, & Moller, 2001; Snowden & Boone, 2007). It does not take great skill to blindly follow orders or directives from superiors. There is little added value to any leadership team from members who don't contribute new ideas or alternative ways of thinking about goals, objectives, or the strategies needed to reach those objectives. The ability to lead is not just the ability to influence and impact those who work beside the assistant principal or report to the assistant principal on an organizational chart; it is the ability to influence and impact members of the organization with more power or those external to the organization who play key roles in the organization's overall effectiveness and mission. This ability to "lead up," to build commitment and support from members of the organization with more position power, will be discussed further in chapter 8. Suffice it to say, assistant principals with impact on the organization are skilled at leading up the organization. It is not that assistant principals are most impactful when they are in agreement with the principal; they are most impactful when they are not in agreement and are able to lead the principal to a superior course of action or thinking on the issue at hand. That is loyalty to the principal.

The Good Cop, Bad Cop Trap

The "good cop, bad cop" trap deals with how the principal and assistant principal handle conflict or bad news within the organization. No leader wants conflict or confrontation with any school stakeholder. Today's leaders are trained in communication skills and in collaborative problem solving. Conflict within the school is often seen as a sign of incompetence or organizational weakness. It is inevitable, however, that conflict will arise and difficult decisions will be made that are unpopular with certain constituencies. How these decisions are communicated and who communicates them says a great deal about the principal–assistant principal team dynamic. A common behavior involving leadership teams

in which there is a clear distinction in position power, as is the case with
the school principal and assistant principal, is for the team member with
the greatest position power to delegate tasks that are unpleasant to team
subordinates. This "good cop, bad cop" approach to communication is
dangerous to the effectiveness of the assistant principal and diminishes
the principal's ability to have every member of the team viewed not just
as problem identifiers but as problem solvers. When the principal becomes the sole deliverer of good news and the assistant principal is the
leader who delivers unpopular or unpleasant news, an unhealthy team
dynamic is in play. When the principal asks the assistant principal to
handle clearly complex and controversial issues within the school so that
the principal can have plausible deniability regarding the decision-making process or the decision itself, an unhealthy team dynamic is in play.
When the assistant principal is tasked with announcing decisions and
procedures that are later overturned by the principal due to negative
stakeholder reactions, an unhealthy team dynamic is in play.

It is human nature to connect one's feelings about the personality or
leadership style of a person with the types and quality of decisions being
made by that person. When the assistant principal is viewed as the deliverer of bad news or is viewed as someone whose decisions can be
overturned by the principal when pressure is applied, the overall effectiveness of the assistant principal to lead in a positive and productive
way is greatly diminished. While it may seem like a good idea in the
short run to use the assistant principal as the "bad cop" so the principal
can remain above the controversy, in the long run the principal's own
effectiveness is diminished. For any leadership team to reach its potential, each member of the team must be able to process both good news
and bad news for the organization. It is important for the assistant principal and the principal to discuss how to handle difficult news as a team,
not as a delegated duty assigned to any one member of the team. When
the assistant principal sees that he has been placed, as a matter of standard organizational operations, as the "bad cop" in the organization, it is
imperative he takes proactive steps to share his concerns with the principal and discuss alternative communication strategies.

The Principal as Leader, Assistant Principal as Manager Trap

A third common principal–assistant principal relationship trap involves job descriptions and responsibilities assigned to the two roles.
When the principal operates as the sole instructional leader of the school
and the assistant principal operates as the organizational leader or organizational manager of the school, the "principal as leader, assistant principal as manager" trap has occurred. This delegation of managerial job
functions to the assistant principal may be one of the most common and,
thus, most dangerous traps for today's assistant principal. In large secon-

dary school settings, it is common to find the actual assistant principal job description dominated by management tasks rather than instructional tasks. The assistant principal for discipline, the assistant principal for facilities, the assistant principal for budget, or the assistant principal for testing are common job titles in secondary schools. In elementary school settings with smaller administrative and support staffs, the tendency to assign management functions to the assistant principal so the principal can be "freed up" to serve as the instructional leader of the school is commonplace.

Clearly management tasks need to be handled. They are often prerequisites to effective teaching and learning. Unorganized schools and schools that are unsafe or poorly managed rarely are schools with happy teachers and academically productive students (Blum, 2005; Cornell & Mayer, 2010). Management tasks are necessary and time consuming but not wholly sufficient for school effectiveness and productivity. It is reasonable for many of these tasks to be assigned to the assistant principal. What is not reasonable or effective, however, is for these tasks to dominate the workday of the assistant principal to the point that she has no opportunity to serve as an instructional leader. If more than half of the assistant principal's workday is consumed with organizing and managing daily operations, her potential to serve as a school leader is greatly diminished. If more than half of the assistant principal's workday is committed to noninstructional activity, she is working at a job in which she is overeducated and overpaid. While the principal may believe he must assign the majority of school management to the assistant principal so the principal can attend to leading teaching and learning, in reality, the time dedicated to effective instructional leadership is only diminished by removing the assistant principal from an instructional leadership role. In cases where the assistant principal serves as a manager and the principal as a leader, the principal becomes isolated, less collaborative, and less impacted by the expertise and leadership that can be provided by the assistant principal as a colleague on the instructional leadership team. There are clearly limits to the workday and workweek. There are practical constraints that make setting aside the time needed to lead difficult. Both assistant principals and principals can easily fall into habits that result in management tasks overwhelming instructional leadership tasks. Specific strategies are needed to create time to lead and to set aside at least half of the workday to focus on teaching and learning within the school. These strategies are discussed in chapter 9.

The complexity and sheer volume of both leadership and management tasks faced by principals and assistant principals can only be tackled by agreeing to delegate certain tasks and divide primary responsibilities for specific aspects of school operations. The assistant principal may be in charge of leading the Parent-Teacher Association, while the principal may take the primary role in leading faculty meetings. Teacher leaders will also play primary roles in leading curriculum development or professional training. The key to establishing the organizational structure of the school, of establishing who has the primary responsibility for what, is collaboration in developing and transparently implementing the organizational structure of the school.

While all of the relationship traps that can befall a principal–assistant principal team are serious and can diminish the effectiveness of the assistant principal as an individual and the leadership team as a whole, the tendency for the assistant principal to become the administrator who manages the school instead of serving as an effective member of the instructional leadership team is the most common and most dangerous trap for both the principal and the assistant principal. It is important for the principal to recognize the tendency for this type of job distribution to occur and work to protect and support the assistant principal's role as an instructional leader. Effective principals who are fortunate enough to have one or more assistant principals on their staff recognize it is a waste of talent and isolating to turn that assistant principal into a school manager. It is also important for the assistant principal to take responsibility for managing his workday so that instructional leadership job functions are a priority.

TWO

Managing Change in the Principalship

In an era of ever-increasing school accountability and pressure to produce strong standardized test scores, having a school principal who spends a career at one school site is a less and less common occurrence. While principal turnover is greatest in high school settings and schools at all levels with at-risk student populations, even in affluent settings the average tenure for an elementary school principal is just five years. The average tenure for today's high school principal is approximately three years (Fuller & Young, 2009). Research not only shows an increase in the number of principals serving shorter and shorter tenures in any one school, it also shows a direct correlation between principal turnover and student achievement. When it comes to student performance, the arrival of a new principal typically accompanies a short-term fall in student achievement (Béteille, Kalogrides, & Loeb 2012; Miller 2009). In some cases it may take up to five years for a new principal to fully implement instructional leadership policies and practices that impact student academic performance. For students in the school, that impact may be five years too late.

In medium- to large-size school districts there is often a rapid turnover not just of school principals but of school district superintendents as well. According to the Education Commission of the States (n.d.), the average tenure of an urban school superintendent in 2008 was just 3.5 years. Superintendents, like principals and teachers, face constant pressure to raise standardized test scores and often look to school-based leadership changes as the fastest way to turn around struggling schools. For these reasons and many more, school districts across the country find themselves working with a constant turnover of school leaders even though a stable, albeit high performing, principal will facilitate student learning, while constant principal turnover will inhibit student learning.

In schools with high principal turnover but stability in the assistant principal position, there are significant opportunities for the assistant principal. An assistant principal familiar with the school can help the new principal become acclimated to the school culture, understand the academic challenges and strengths inherent in the school, and shorten the typical time needed to fully realize her objectives as the new instructional leader in the school. With the support and expertise of a high performing assistant principal who is currently serving at the school, it should not take five years for a new principal to realize her full potential in the school. How the assistant principal reacts to the new school leader and what the assistant principal does and does not do as a key figure in the new leadership team in the school will go a long way in determining both the ultimate success of the new principal and the amount of time needed for that success to occur. It is difficult to overstate the power and importance of building strong professional relationships with the principal and the faculty in order to be a successful and effective leader (Avolio, 1999; Goleman, 2000).

There are a number of reasons a superintendent will change principals at a school. The sitting principal may be retiring or taking another job within the organization. The superintendent may feel it is time for a change of leadership style in order to better meet the needs of the school and the community. Decisions to make a principal change at a school, while a direct responsibility of the superintendent, are typically not made in isolation. Both internal and external stakeholders in the school community will have opinions regarding the need for the change, the process used to arrive at the change, and the leadership style expected of the individual selected to be the new principal. Many stakeholders want a voice in the selection of the new school principal, and many stakeholders will certainly have opinions regarding the selection process and outcome.

There will also be a great deal of teacher anxiety about the leadership style of the new principal and the new goals, objectives, and school procedures that principal may bring. If the relationship between the principal and the faculty is critical to the climate and culture of the school, this change has the potential to change the overall climate of the school for the better, or for the worse. Anxiety regarding the reasons for a change in the school principal and the individual selected to be the school principal is not limited to the school faculty or other school stakeholders; it is also present in the assistant principal preparing to work with a new leader.

How, then, can the sitting assistant principal serve as a positive change agent and facilitate the work of this new principal and the administrative leadership team so that stakeholder anxiety is reduced and student achievement is maintained or accelerated? Should the assistant principal be proactive by sharing as much institutional memory as possible with the principal? Should the assistant principal work to make sure that existing procedures within the school are maintained so that any changes made are steady and incremental? Should the assistant principal try to mold the new principal to be like the old boss in those areas of leadership that were popular with the faculty and community and assure that negatively perceived behaviors are not part of the new leadership style? How the assistant principal responds to these questions will go a long way toward establishing the tone of the relationship between the assistant principal and the principal. How these issues are resolved will also impact the culture and climate in the school for all stakeholders.

PRINCIPAL EXPECTATIONS

It is not just the faculty, community stakeholders, and existing assistant principal who face anxiety and expectations regarding the new principal. The new principal also comes to the job with certain anxieties and expectations. The principal's expectations for the assistant principal, the key lieutenant in the principal's leadership team, must be understood by the assistant principal. While all principals, just like any educator in the school, have unique personal backgrounds and professional experiences, there is usually a common job description and set of organizational objectives that most principals, be they first-year appointees or seasoned veterans, bring to the position. When the assistant principal recognizes that the new principal is a unique individual with a specific sets of skills and experiences but also shares a common mission and set of objectives for the school, there is a clear opportunity to begin the principal–assistant principal relationship with a focus on that common mission and set of objectives.

Be a Partner

The new principal needs to establish a unique, comfortable approach to problem solving and communication. Above all else, the new principal is looking for the assistant principal to be a trusted, high performing partner. As the assistant principal, it is important to spend as much time as possible with the new principal to facilitate the establishment of that partnership so there is an understanding of the principal's approaches to leadership, problem solving, and communication. This time together will also give the assistant principal an opportunity to show the principal what he does for a living, what his own skill set is. Time together also helps to build that most important attribute of a successful partnership: trust.

Be a Teacher

For every new principal, knowledge and understanding of the school's history, culture, climate, academic successes, and challenges are key to making the best decisions possible. One of the first jobs the high performing assistant principal can perform for the new principal is that of teacher. The assistant principal working as a teacher to the principal can explain current job functions, job responsibilities, and job histories of the leadership team within the administration, the faculty, and the support staff. It is imperative that the assistant principal facilitate, in every way possible, the principal's understanding of the existing school culture and climate, as well as the successes and challenges the school is currently facing. The new principal needs to understand every aspect of the school from the perspective of the highest ranking administrator in the school, the sitting assistant principal. The assistant principal should be proactive in sharing this institutional memory and expertise regarding what is and is not working in the school. Effective principals know they cannot lead a school alone or understand all the history and social dynamics at play without honest feedback from trusted colleagues. Principals are grateful to have assistant principals who are proactive. At the same time that a complete and open description of the current health of the school community is provided, it is also important for the assistant principal to recognize that what is being shared is a point of view from one perspective. The effective assistant principal makes it clear to the principal that the information and perspective being given represents the assistant principal's best thinking but that this perspective is just one of many perspectives held by school stakeholders. There will be different points of view from other stakeholders, and the principal must seek out and hear those divergent points of view in order to get a complete picture of the school culture. In fact, the assistant principal should be a key player in identifying what those points of view are and who shares those differing points of view to facilitate the principal's ability to communicate with key stakeholders. The effective assistant principal is not trying to tell the new principal what to think but rather what the assistant principal thinks, as well as describing those stakeholders in and outside of the organization who may have differing opinions.

It is also a mistake for assistant principals to try to turn new principals into a replica of their predecessors, even if that predecessor was highly respected and high performing. The effective assistant principal recognizes and respects the fact that the new principal arrives with a unique approach and process for leading. The new principal also arrives with a specific set of goals and objectives that have most likely been articulated by the superintendent. The effective assistant principal is teaching the principal all that is known about the school, not attempting to change the principal's style or organizational goals but to provide the principal with as much institutional knowledge as possible.

Be a Listener

Principals also value the ability of the assistant principal to listen and understand. A key component in all effective communication is the ability to be a good listener (Nahavandi, 2006; Riggio & Reichard, 2008). Establishing an effective and high performing leadership relationship with a new principal requires more than sharing information, experiences, and opinions regarding the current state of the school community; it requires being a good listener. The assistant principal should be an observer, a monitor, and a frequent questioner with one specific goal in mind: discovering what matters most to the new principal. What are the goals and the procedures the new principal wants to implement in order to reach those goals? What information will support the principal in terms of accomplishing the aspirations and dreams for the school as a whole? The assistant principal cannot support the principal's goals if they are not clearly understood. The assistant principal cannot implement new policies and procedures on behalf of the principal if those goals and procedures are not understood. The assistant principal cannot effectively articulate the principal's vision to stakeholders if the assistant principal has not truly heard and understood that vision. The assistant principal can support the new principal by being a good listener to the faculty, students, staff, and other stakeholders as they also adapt to the new leadership within the school. The high performing assistant principal is also listening and understanding the concerns and areas of agreement regarding changes being made by the new principal and sharing those concerns with the principal in a way that maintains trust between the assistant principal and school stakeholders. The skills and strategies needed by the assistant principal to maintain trust and loyalty with all the school's stakeholders will be discussed further in chapter 5.

Be a Learner

In addition to being a good listener, the assistant principal should also be a keen observer of the principal's leadership style. The goal for the assistant principal is to create an effective, high performing leadership team with the principal. While it is important for the assistant principal to know and keep a unique leadership voice (more on this in chapter 3), in order to be a genuine and effective leader for the long run, the assistant principal must also understand that one critical job responsibility is to learn and demonstrate an approach to leadership and problem solving that is congruent with the principal's approach.

The new principal will bring many changes to the school. The new principal will bring new expertise and experience to the school that provides an opportunity for the proactive assistant principal to learn new strategies. The arrival of a new principal is a great opportunity for the assistant principal to teach by sharing knowledge and experiences gained as a leader in the school; and this is also a great opportunity for the assistant principal to learn and be mentored by a new leader. Every new principal brings a new opportunity for the assistant principal to expand leadership skills, to see the school through new eyes, to learn new ways of problem solving and communicating. High performing principals want to mentor other educators. Principals want to make a difference not just in the lives of their students but also in the lives of their colleagues. Effective assistant principals see the arrival of a new principal not as a threat or a burden but as an opportunity: an opportunity to share their expertise and an opportunity to learn from the expertise of the principal.

The assistant principal should also seek to learn and understand the expectations the principal has for the working relationship between the principal and the assistant principal and how best to meet those exceptions on behalf of the principal.

In addition to bringing new experiences and approaches to leadership that can serve as valuable learning opportunities for the assistant principal, the new principal may very well bring changes that include a change in the job responsibilities for the assistant principal. When these changes to the job description or the organizational practices between the principal and the assistant principal occur, the effective assistant principal works hard to function as a loyal and trusting partner to the principal. The most effective assistant principal will learn these new job roles and implement them with fidelity. This will be done while still leading in those areas of responsibility that remain the same. In chapter 9, "The 50 Percent Rule," specific strategies for managing and prioritizing time effectively are discussed that can support the assistant principal tasked with handling multiple job roles. The high performing assistant principal does not want to be a specialist but a generalist, an instructional leader who is capable and experienced in all school operations. The effective assistant principal sees every new job role as a new opportunity to learn another system or subsystem within the school structure. Regardless of the area of responsibility assigned, the assistant principal needs to remain proactive, maintain a positive orientation toward the work, and learn the strategies and skills necessary to be the very best in that job role even when assigned to job responsibilities that may be limited in scope or have changed as a result of new leadership. How can the assistant principal support the new principal? By being a great teacher to that principal and a great student of that principal.

Assistant Principal Expectations

Just as the new principal expects support from the assistant principal by being an effective partner, teacher, listener, and learner, it is also important and reasonable for the incumbent assistant principal to have professional expectations for the new principal. Partnerships are teams, and effective teams bring value to, and receive value from, everyone on the team. It is not coincidental that the expectations and aspirations the principal has regarding the assistant principal are similar to the expectations the assistant principal should have and articulate to the principal. It is not just assistant principals receiving new teammates; the principals are also teaming with new assistant principals and need to know their expectations.

Be a Partner

Just as the sitting assistant principal has an obligation to partner with and support the new principal, the new principal also has an obligation to support the assistant principal already in the building. For the assistant principal to be an effective leader and partner with the new principal, faculty, students, and other stakeholders in the school must see the principal publicly and privately supporting the work and value of the assistant principal. It is not in the principal's best interest to give the impression that the assistant principal is not valued or capable of independent decision making. As the assistant principal welcoming a new principal, a new boss, it is appropriate to articulate partnership hopes and expectations of support from the principal.

Be a Mentor

It is also important for the principal to serve as a mentor to the assistant principal. The assistant principal cannot learn from a principal who is not willing to teach. As the assistant principal, it is appropriate to articulate hopes and expectations for mentoring. A principal who has been through the vetting process and handpicked to serve as the instructional leader for a new school will typically be the type of leader who appreciates the desire of the assistant principal to learn and grow as a professional. It is also flattering and affirming to have subordinates asking and seeking the boss's guidance and words of wisdom. As the assistant principal reporting to a new principal, have the discussion with the principal about the needs and hopes for a partnership that includes mentoring.

THREE

Finding and Keeping Your Unique Leadership Voice

Today's school leader, whether it is the principal, the assistant principal, or a teacher leader, cannot rely on position power alone to accomplish organizational goals and objectives. Our schools are open and dynamic social systems with many internal and external constituencies. Effective schools are learning communities that operate in a collaborative fashion in a climate of mutual trust and respect rather than in a hierarchal fashion that relies on directives and dictates from superiors in the state house, the district office, or the principal's office. Effective schools are goal and outcome oriented and operate best when the adults in the building are working collaboratively to reach those goals.

To lead in a collaborative fashion, to lead a community of learners, to lead in the open social system that is today's modern school, the assistant principal must develop a "leadership voice" focused on learning for both the students and adults in the school (DuFour, 2002). Having a voice that is consistent and is grounded in a set of leadership values will allow the assistant principal to work effectively as a team member for the faculty and with the principal, while still maintaining an independent place and purpose within the school organization. Too often, assistant principals lose their own identity in an attempt to serve as a clone of the principal or as an honorary member of the school faculty. Neither approach will serve the assistant principal well. Neither approach will result in respect from the faculty or the principal.

In order to lead effectively, the assistant principal must build a unique expert and charismatic power. In order to lead effectively,

the assistant principal must set aside position power as the means to lead. High impact assistant principals want to be experts in teaching and learning; they want to be instructional experts. Instructional experts know the best practices for teaching and learning. They stay current and remain lifelong learners themselves. When it comes to teaching and learning, instructional leaders practice what they preach. It is not that the instructional expert knows all the answers to the complex world of teaching and learning in twenty-first-century modern education, it is that the instructional expert wants to know the answers to teaching and learning. This commitment to learning gives rise to a voice as a leader worth listening to and following. This commitment to learning is charismatic and encourages, by example, other educators to follow.

In addition to a commitment to expertise, to knowing what you are talking about, is the commitment to finding a leadership style that is both effective and true to your leadership philosophy. How does the assistant principal view the role of the faculty in the leadership of a school? What rights and responsibilities do students have in the assistant principal's expectations for how the school will function? How does the assistant principal view parents, business leaders, and other external stakeholders' roles in school governance and reporting? The answer to these questions and many more like them determines the unique voice and leadership philosophy of the assistant principal. In each case, the answers and effectiveness of the assistant principal will not be in just what the assistant principal says but also in how the assistant principal leads. Every assistant principal's unique leadership voice will be heard by all the stakeholders in and outside the school with every action taken. When those actions are inclusive rather than exclusive, when they are consistently aligned with the mission of the school and are in the best interest of the adults and students in the building, when they foster a community of goal-oriented learners, the assistant principal's charismatic power rises. To be charismatic does not have to mean one is a dynamic public speaker or a larger than life presence in the room. This charisma comes from being authentic about how every child in the school is valued. This charisma comes from assistant principal actions that over time consistently show a level of respect and desire to collaborate with teachers and all school stakeholders.

When the assistant principal has expert power, has charismatic power, has a "sense of self" as a collaborative leader, that assistant principal has a leadership voice that will be heard and respected by all stakeholders in the school community.

POSITION POWER AND LEADERSHIP VOICE

Too often, however, when assistant principals are beginning their career, the trappings that come with that first promotion to assistant principal lead the assistant principal to rely on this newfound power to be their voice as a leader. A new job and title, increased compensation and responsibility, the attainment of a long-term goal to get an advanced degree, and a promotion to administration all are part of the significant accomplishment of becoming an assistant principal, of becoming a school leader. Too often assistant principals want to prove quickly that they have what it takes to accomplish goals and objectives for the principal and the school. The use of position power can appear to be an effective and fast way of accomplishing those institutional and personal goals. After all, the position of assistant principal comes with a level of authority and power; why not use it?

While the power of position comes with the job, developing a reputation as a lifelong learner, as an expert in the field of school leadership, takes time. Developing a reputation as a charismatic individual who cares deeply about the success of all the students in the school and the teachers who educate them also takes time. It seems so much easier and faster to simply use the power vested in the position to move the organization along toward its goals. The biggest problem with this approach to leadership is that it doesn't work. The assistant principal who relies exclusively on position power to accomplish tasks will fail to accomplish goals, and the leader whose voice, style, and reputation are associated with position power will be viewed negatively inside and outside of the organization. All assistant principals have position power. The best assistant principals rarely have to use it.

Advanced Degrees and Lifelong Learning

A common prerequisite for becoming an assistant principal is the attainment of an advanced degree. Often a master's in educational leadership or a master's in curriculum and instruction is required for the job. Most educators earn these degrees while working full-time jobs and/or raising a family. The degree can be expensive and time consuming and also requires a commitment to learning on the part of the graduate student. The awarding of the degree is, in and of itself, a signature accomplishment that only small fractions of the population ever achieve. There is a natural sense of accomplishment and completion. Too often, however, as the assistant principal begins the role of school leader, the role of lifelong learner retreats to the back burner or disappears all together. After all, an advanced degree has just been completed; state licensing exams have been passed; and there is work to be done to learn the new role of instructional leader and to accomplish the many tasks assigned. It is all too easy for the assistant principal to feel that there is neither the time nor the need to continue to learn. The problem, again, with this approach is that it doesn't work. In fact, the longer you serve as an assistant principal relying on yesterday's knowledge and learning, the farther you are from having the leadership voice of an expert. If education best practices are constantly changing, the expert educational leader must be constantly learning. As a lifelong learner committed to impacting in a positive way the quality of teaching and learning that occurs in the school, the high performing assistant principal should join the local, state, and national professional organizations that are dedicated to improving education. In order to remain a lifelong learner and maintain currency in the field, the assistant principal should read the latest books on subjects such as school leadership, instructional design, and teacher evaluation. For a partial list of some of the national organizations that assistant principals should join, see the appendix of this book.

THE PRINCIPAL AND LEADERSHIP VOICE

Clearly there are great opportunities and great challenges assistant principals face when working with their direct supervisor, the principal. One of those challenges can be discord or lack of alignment between the philosophy of education and leadership that makes up the leadership style of the assistant principal and the leadership style of the principal. The good news is that this lack of alignment is not common and does not have to be an insurmountable obstacle to either the principal–assistant principal relationship or the relationship between the faculty and school administration. School leadership is usually viewed by district administrators as a leadership team. These teams are selected to work together and to augment each other's leadership styles and strengths. The placement of the principal in a specific school is not a random event. The placement of the assistant principal in a school is not a random event. These placements are made by district leadership, with feedback from many stakeholders both within and outside the formal school structure. These placements typically take into consideration the strengths and experiences that each member of the school administrative team bring to the job.

When assistant principals do find themselves, however, working for a principal with a very different leadership style and voice, they should not fall into the trap of believing they must either be true to their own leadership voice in a way that will cause dissention or change their own style of leadership and become a clone of the principal. The effective assistant principal does the following to stay true to who they are as an educational leader while supporting the principal they are assigned to:

1. Discuss your leadership style and the underlying philosophy that guides that style with your principal. Identify the strengths you believe your leadership voice brings to the administrative team, to the faculty, and to the goals and objectives the principal has for the school.
2. Learn the leadership style and underlying philosophy that guides your principal. What are the strengths that this style brings to the

school? How can your leadership strengths and your principal's leadership strengths further the mission of the school? You do not need to be the principal's clone to be effective or supportive. You do, however, need to understand and reach a consensus with your principal regarding the leadership differences and strengths that you each have and how, as a team, you will interact with each other and with the faculty as instructional leaders relying on more than position power.

3. Share these discussions of style and diverse strengths with your faculty. They are part of the leadership team as well. When the faculty knows that there is a degree of self-awareness and self-reflection between the principal and the assistant principal regarding leadership styles, that the assistant principal is not a clone of the principal but a respected colleague with a unique personality and leadership strengths, the faculty will not only tolerate those differences, they will respect both the assistant principal and the principal for practicing the same collaborative and facilitative approach with each other that they seek from the faculty toward accomplishing the objectives of the school.

The teachers and administrators in every school expect diverse groups of students to learn from and respect each other and function as a team. Parents and administrators in every school expect diverse faculty to learn from each other, to support a common mission for their school, and to support each other in working toward that mission. So, too, the principal and assistant principal should be expected to merge disparate leadership styles and strengths into a unified team.

STANDARDS OF EVIDENCE AND LEADERSHIP VOICE

All educators are impacted in profound ways by their own experiences. What each stakeholder in the school community has witnessed firsthand, whether as a former student in school, a teacher, a parent, a graduate student, or members of the community, all of these experiences impact the assumptions and conclusions that are reached about teaching and learning. Everyone's experiences shape and inform a worldview, including the assistant principal's. The effective assistant principal recognizes that these experiences have helped to shape a unique leadership voice in ways that are both positive and negative. The effective assistant principal also recognizes, however, that personal experiences are limited in scope and do not necessarily represent a clear and complete picture of either the people involved in schooling or the processes used to educate children in schools.

An important question the assistant principal, as a school leader, should ask is, what are the limitations to the personal experiences brought to the job and what are the standards of evidence used to shape and inform future experiences and opinions? The assistant principal who builds a belief system regarding what works and what doesn't as an instructional leader around limited personal experiences or anecdotes from colleagues is not demonstrating expert power. Too often, a teacher or a school leader will decide that students from poverty, for example, cannot learn at the highest levels, because it has been their personal experience that these students, with whom they interacted in the past in some capacity, did not learn at the highest level. Perhaps the teacher or leader has heard from others who also worked with high poverty students, and they were not successful either. Experiences alone do not represent a strong enough standard on which to build a set of guiding principles for leadership. Those guiding principles should be built on a strong preponderance of data and evidence gathered over time by other experts in the field.

Keeping Your Leadership Voice

The American Dream is deeply rooted in the concept of upward mobility as an indicator of success and accomplishment (Sawhill & Morton, 2007; Hill & Torres, 2010). The higher up the ladder in any profession one goes, the greater the recognition, both financially and socially, that individual expects to receive. American schools are not immune from this cultural value and expectation.

Many superintendents and principals actively pursue and hire leaders who want to move up the ladder, who are hungry for the next promotion and are motivated by the desire to be promoted as quickly as possible. There is certainly nothing wrong with these aspirational behaviors. We will examine them in some detail in chapter 14. The problem with connecting an identity, a sense of self, and a sense of organizational worth to the next promotion is the inevitable catch-22 built into any pyramidal organizational structure. Today's school structure is hierarchical. The higher up the organizational structure an individual goes, the fewer jobs there will be. There are more teachers in every school than there are administrators. There are more school-based administrators in every district than there are district-based administrators working in the central office, and there are more assistant principals in every district than there are principals. It is not at all uncommon for a school district, regardless of its size, to have two to three times the number of assistant principals as principal positions. Look at the personnel charts for any district. Look at the number of school principals and the number of school assistant principals. The math alone dictates that two-thirds of all assistant principals will be career assistant principals and will never be promoted to the position of school principal.

Does this mean that the majority of assistant principals should be viewed by their superiors as failures or should view themselves as failures if they are never promoted to principal? Does this mean that all principals who are not eventually promoted to high ranking district administrative positions should also be viewed as failures? If every assistant principal must become, or seek to become, a principal in order to be viewed as a successful and high performing leader, does the same hold true for teachers? Should every teacher in every school aspire to be an assistant principal in order to be perceived as high performing and impactful? Is the career of teacher, or of assistant principal, less valuable than the career of a principal? Ask a student or an adult about who impacted them in school or made a difference in their life. Odds are the response will be the name of one particular educator or adult in the building; that adult could be the principal, a particular teacher, an assistant principal, or the custodian or school secretary. One thing is certain: the impact felt by that child and remembered through life will not be connected to the title or power of the adult but the behavior of the adult.

If the view of leadership in a school district is that only upwardly mobile individuals have true passion for the work and the ability to lead and impact students in positive and profound ways, that is a culture destined to lower the morale and effectiveness of most of the leadership workforce in the district: the district's teachers and assistant principals. It is a recipe for isolation and a roadblock for collaboration. The effective school culture is not shaped like a pyramid, with position power determining who the leaders are. The effective school culture is built on collaboration, expert power and facilitative leadership. While the organizational structure of school systems may resemble a pyramid, the high performing assistant principal works to make the operational structure more of a circle, more a learning community than a top-down hierarchy. The effective school system recognizes leadership where it is found, whether that is within the school faculty or the school assistant principal.

The assistant principal's voice as an instructional leader is not contingent on any promotion. The assistant principal's power to be an effective leader is not dependent on the power and authority that comes with the title of assistant principal or the potential to be a principal in the future. Leadership authority comes from the power granted to the assistant principal by colleagues based on expertise, charisma, trust, collaboration—in short, on the leadership skills that are possessed, not on the leadership title on the office door. No one becomes an effective leader simply by being the assistant principal or the principal but rather by exhibiting leadership skills on a consistent basis. An important way for the assistant principal to keep a leadership voice is to separate job promotion aspirations from a sense of self-worth or accomplishment.

A second obstacle to maintaining a voice as an instructional leader within the school is the all too common tendency for the assistant principal's role to be seen as a management role rather than a leadership role, as discussed in chapter 1. This viewpoint can come from both the principal and the faculty and is a common trap for the assistant principal. Too often, assistant principals are assigned to and "settle" for administrative roles that, while necessary and expected by the principal and the organization in general, are not roles that involve instructional leadership. To keep a true leadership voice, the assistant principal must attend to the more mundane management obligations in the job description and attend to those job responsibilities with pride and purpose. These managerial assistant principal job functions are a prerequisite for school success and the assistant principal's own individual success. Poorly managed schools cannot be quality led schools. In order to become an instructional leader, however, assistant principals must also establish themselves as leaders in curriculum, instruction, assessment, and professional development, in addition to any school operations or management level job responsibilities that have been assigned. It is easy for the assistant principal to become office bound or bound to managerial tasks, as opposed to instructional leadership tasks that impact teaching and learning. It is easy for both the faculty and the principal to delegate the many necessary, but time consuming, organizational tasks they face to the assistant principal. What is hard, but necessary, is for the assistant principal to handle all of these delegated tasks while at the same time maintaining a leadership role in the primary missions of the school: teaching and learning. In chapter 9 we will discuss ways to address these management tasks while still creating time to be an instructional leader. The effective assistant principal must work on a daily basis to not fall victim to the false dichotomy of the assistant principal as a school manager or the assistant principal as a school leader. The effective assistant principal has to be both.

II

The Faculty Partner

FOUR

Expert Power versus Position Power

Becoming as assistant principal is an outstanding accomplishment. Advanced degrees have been earned, state licensing exams have been passed, successful interviews with a variety of internal and external stakeholders have occurred, in-box activities have been completed, and portfolios have been developed, all resulting in school leaders at the highest level identifying the assistant principal as a leader in the field of P–12 education. Just one quick review of any assistant principal job description will make it clear that the scope, responsibility, and accountability called for within the position are daunting.

Clearly, with responsibility comes authority. While in the past some assistant principal job descriptions may have been limited to management responsibilities only, today's modern assistant principal job description will include evaluating teachers, which requires the assistant principal to determine the overall quality and effectiveness of classroom instruction and to complete annual summative reports on teacher effectiveness that can impact teacher job retention as well as compensation. The assistant principal often has the power to assign teachers to specific classrooms, determining who goes to the portables and who is in the new wing of the building. The assistant principal builds master schedules, manages the allocation of funds, decides on appropriate disciplinary action regarding student behavior, and completes a wide variety of additional tasks that are a result of the power of the position. This power is delegated to the assistant principal by the organization as a function of the job. The power is real and is there for a reason. School systems tend to default toward a hierarchy of authority and a bureaucratic organizational structure for the purpose of accountability and responsibility to both internal and external stakeholders (Bates, 1980). School systems want to establish the scope of the work to be accomplished by its members.

33

Contracts are written and agreed to with employees for this very purpose; to outline who is responsible for what, to establish who has the authority to do what.

What are not inherent, however, in any list of powers authorized by the position are the power to motivate or influence people or the power that comes with expertise in the field. Job titles, the organizational structure, and the power that comes with those titles and structures, in and of themselves, do not guarantee effective leadership. In fact, leaders who rely solely on the power of the position to accomplish tasks are typically not effective in complex systems like schools. To be more specific, what the use of position power cannot do effectively is build trust or a sense of collaboration with students, teachers, or any other stakeholders for that matter. In fact, in today's complex school environment, position power is rarely effective in even yielding compliance from stakeholders (Hargreaves & Fink, 2004). While it may seem easier and quicker to use the authority vested in the power of the position, the use of position power to accomplish organizational goals and objectives should be relegated to two purposes only: first, the safety of the students and adults in the building and, second, the implementation of routine management tasks regarding the daily operations of the building.

POSITION POWER AND SCHOOL SAFETY

First, use the position power that comes with the title of assistant principal when student and staff safety are at risk. Whenever an issue regarding safety for any stakeholder occurs, whether it is physical safety or emotional safety, use the power of the position to act in a timely and appropriate manner. The work that leads up to implementing the protocols to maintain student and staff safety must be done collaboratively. It takes expert power and teamwork to develop the best practices needed to ensure as safe an environment as possible. All stakeholders should be involved in learning the best practices for maintaining a safe environment and identifying areas of concern. The development of curriculum and action plans for reducing bullying on campus or building the capacity for tolerance and respect among all school community members should be led by the principal and the assistant principal through a collaborative process. When issues of school safety actually occur, however, it is imperative that school leaders, leaders like the assistant principal, act quickly and decisively. Student safety is a prerequisite for student learning (Haynes, Emmons, & Ben-Avie, 1997; Chen & Weikart, 2008). There is no more important leadership responsibility than maintaining a physically and emotionally safe school environment for everyone. When it comes to the well-being of everyone in the school, it is imperative that leaders use the power of the position to act when needed.

POSITION POWER AND ROUTINE MANAGEMENT TASKS

Second, use position power to accomplish, in an efficient manner, the routine tasks of managing school operations. The school day is filled with a myriad of interactions often requiring decisions to be made and tasks to be assigned. Not every decision requires the formation of a committee. Not every issue can wait for stakeholder feedback. Teachers have no interest in having their very busy schedules constantly interrupted to handle or advise on routine management decisions. Well-meaning assistant principals who are committed to a collaborative form of leadership can lose their effectiveness as leaders if every issue, every decision, no matter how mundane, becomes an agenda item for the next faculty meeting. It is a common mistake for assistant principals to turn faculty or departmental meetings that could be used to explore significant instructional issues or develop professional practices into "administrivia" meetings. High performing assistant principals use the power and responsibility they have been given to handle routine management tasks efficiently and consistently. These are the tasks that both the principal and the faculty expect the assistant principal to handle unilaterally; these are the tasks that allow the school to run efficiently. The leadership skill that the assistant principal must have is the ability to know which of the many tasks and decision points encountered on a daily basis are routine and mundane and which have the potential to impact teaching and learning and, thus, should be handled collaboratively. To some extent, experience on the job and past practice and expectations from both the principal and the faculty will help determine which decisions involve routine daily operations and can be handled unilaterally and which require collaboration. One easy way to answer the question of whether an issue requires a routine management decision or instructional leadership decision is to ask the following question: Does this decision in any meaningful way impact the curriculum, instruction, assessment, professional development activities or objectives within the school? If the answer to that question is yes, use expert power and collaborative power rather than position power to arrive at the decision.

As discussed earlier, the position of assistant principal does come with power. While that power has been earned and, as discussed, should be used to maintain safety and handle routine tasks, the overuse of the power of the position can be counterproductive for the assistant principal. Just because a position comes with authority and the occupant of the position is entitled to exercise that authority, it does not mean the authority, the power of the position, should always be used. The sense that a leader is entitled to unilateral decision making because of the authority vested in the position held is one of the most common and dangerous leadership traps there is. When the assistant principal feels entitled to the power of the position, leadership ineffectiveness is sure to follow.

THE ENTITLEMENT TRAP

It is easy to fall into the position power entitlement trap. The assistant principal is, in fact, entitled to use the authority vested within the job description. As discussed earlier, a great deal of work and sacrifice went into earning the position of assistant principal, and the accomplishment is very real. It is human nature to want to exercise this newly acquired power, to take it for a test drive. It is also tempting for assistant principals to want to show the principal and the teachers that they are no longer a member of the faculty but are now part of the administrative team. The use of the power assigned to the position can be an easy way to demonstrate this change in organizational status to colleagues and superiors. The position of assistant principal comes with significant and specific job responsibilities. It is easy to fall back on the power of the position as a way to mandate or dictate the processes and procedures one wants to see implemented in order to accomplish the tasks assigned. After all, school leaders are hired to make decisions.

Although discussed earlier, it's worth repeating that the use of position power as a means to accomplish complex organizational objectives, to improve teaching and learning in today's schools, doesn't work (Harris, 2002). Even worse, the use of position power as the mechanism to attempt to build effective schools is counterproductive. The school and its stakeholders would be better off if the assistant principal did nothing as opposed to relying on the power of the job to force compliance toward school goals. The reality of the effective use of position power is this: avoiding this sense of entitlement and the use of position-related power as a means for accomplishing goals is critical to actually accomplishing those goals. It may sound counterintuitive, but the best use of the power of the position of assistant principal is not to use it. Effective assistant principals build capacity as experts and as collaborators in their fields. Effective assistant principals use charismatic power to build capacity to inspire and motivate others toward that work. Effective assistant principals don't rely on position power; effective assistant principals use expert power and charismatic power to lead.

The Assistant Principal and Expert Power

The research regarding collaborative leadership, building trust within the organization, enhancing the motivation of the teachers and students in the school, and increasing job satisfaction and effectiveness is overwhelming (Hallinger & Heck, 2010). Effective school leaders do not rely on position power to accomplish these objectives; they rely on expert power.

Expert power requires the high performing school leader to be well versed in the profession; to have content knowledge about the pedagogy, policies, and procedures that are expected to be understood and implemented; and to understand the best practices in effective school leadership. Every assistant principal should stay well versed in curriculum, instruction, assessment, and professional development. Assistant principals should have a full understanding of the curriculum in the school, of what students are expected to learn. Assistant principals should have a full understanding of the instructional framework expected of the teachers in the school. Assistant principals should have a full understanding of both the formative and summative assessment systems being used in the school. And finally, assistant principals should understand and implement sound professional development practices so that all the adults in the school are getting better at the curriculum, instruction, and assessment systems being used. School leadership entails more than school management. School leadership requires more than successfully completing job responsibilities and assignments. School leadership requires instructional expertise as well as expertise in communication, motivation, and goal setting. The impactful assistant principal is both an instructional expert and an expert in leadership theory and practice.

Assistant principals do not need to know everything to be considered by stakeholders and colleagues as experts in the field. What all school leaders who are perceived as having expert power do have in common, however, is the desire to know more. Leaders who are seen as experts, as being smart, view learning and growing as a responsibility to the profession, as an effective source of power. The use of position authority as an effective source of power is never effective. In short, leaders with expert power orientations are lifelong learners. What leaders with expert power have is a passion for learning. These leaders don't pretend to know everything. The leader with an excerpt orientation says, "I don't know. Let's go find out." When faculty and other stakeholders see the assistant principal as a leader who wants to know how to be better and how to make everyone else better at educating children, that leader has, and is able to use, expert power to shape and influence others.

The Assistant Principal and Charismatic Power

The Merriam-Webster dictionary (2003) defines charisma as "a personal magic of leadership arousing special popular loyalty or enthusiasm." Often this "magic of leadership" is viewed as synonymous with being an extrovert, someone with a larger than life personality. Even the definition itself defines charisma as having a "magical" orientation, implying charisma as something one is born with, something that is out of one's control. In this view, the leader either has charisma or does not. Charisma is not seen as a leadership skill that can be developed or enhanced.

With all due respect to Merriam-Webster, however, if charisma is defined not as some type of magical power but the ability to motivate and influence the behavior of others, then the ability to be charismatic is not only possible for all leaders to possess but a necessary prerequisite for leadership effectiveness. The charismatic leader does not need magical powers bestowed on them but rather leadership skills that inspire others to follow. The charismatic leader who is able to influence and motivate others does not have to be an extrovert. The introvert with the quiet but ubiquitous determination to make a difference can also be a charismatic leader. If leadership requires collaboration with a wide variety of stakeholders with different personalities and orientations toward how to work effectively as a team, if leadership requires situational awareness and an understanding that no one approach will always work in every situation, then the leader who is always an extrovert will be just as limited as a leader who is always introverted.

The charismatic leader, the leader who has the ability to influence others, is what Daniel Pink (2014) calls an "ambivert." Ambiverts have the ability to harness the power of extroversion with groups of people when needed with the ability to focus and function as an introvert, working alone when needed. Ambiverts are comfortable leading and working in groups and are comfortable leading and working alone. Most leaders, most people, do not have personalities that reside at one end of the extrovert-introvert scale. Most leaders, like everyone else in the organization, fall somewhere in the middle. The leader with charismatic power develops the ability to harness both the effectiveness of introverted behavior with the effectiveness of extroverted behavior to influence the direction of the organization. In many ways, being charismatic is the result of the ability to be self-reflective, to understand when being an extrovert is the most productive approach to solving a complex problem and when being introverted is the best approach. The ability to influence members at all levels of the organization, the ability to motivate others toward a common goal, the ability to build a team with a sense of purpose, a mission—these are all outcomes that high performing leaders seek from the stakeholders in the organization. These are also outcomes that have a greater chance of occurring when the leader develops and uses charismatic power.

FIVE

Building Faculty Trust and Commitment

Chapters 1 and 2 discussed the important components that must exist between the principal and the assistant principal for a successful leadership team. Just as there are critical components to building a trusting relationship with the principal, the assistant principal must also have the skill set to build and earn the trust and respect of the faculty. Perhaps one of the most difficult challenges, and most important requisites for success, for any assistant principal is learning how to maintain open trust and communication with the faculty and still be loyal and communicative with the principal. Chapters 4, 5, and 6 explore the many components that go into the development of the assistant principal as a high impact faculty partner. The issues surrounding the development of faculty trust and respect, however, are not just issues of how the assistant principal interacts with teachers and other stakeholders; they are issues regarding how the administrative team, as a unit, interacts with and is perceived by the faculty.

BUILDING FACULTY PARTNERSHIPS

When it comes to building trust and open communication with the faculty, there are several strategies that can be implemented that will allow the assistant principal to be a partner to, and resource for, the faculty while maintaining the critical leadership partnership with the principal. This ability to be a partner, a trusted advisor, and a leader for both the faculty and the principal is perhaps the greatest challenge faced by today's assistant principal and the greatest opportunity to lead from the middle of the organization and impact both the quality of teaching and of administrative leadership in the building. Three strategies for maintaining this balance between the role of the assistant principal as a faculty partner and as a principal partner are consistency, trust, and transparency.

Bringing faculty issues to the principal, making faculty concerns issues that the assistant principal cares about and acts upon, and making the foundation of all faculty communication transparent will result in faculty trust and commitment to the work the assistant principal is trying to accomplish.

Bringing Faculty Issues to the Principal

Often teachers will look to the assistant principal as someone to confide in about issues impacting the faculty. One or more faculty members may bring a concern to the assistant principal's attention in hopes that the assistant principal can intervene in some fashion, often with the principal, to remedy the situation. This is particularly true if the assistant principal is a visible presence and seen as someone who can be trusted and has the ear of the principal. How should the assistant principal respond to issues the faculty present? How can the assistant principal attend to the issues while still maintaining trust and open communication with both the faculty and the principal?

One strategy is to bring the faculty problem the principal's attention. Not every issue presented to the assistant principal needs to be resolved by the assistant principal. It is true that it is the nature of leadership to want to find solutions to problems. In a very real way, effective leadership is effective solution finding. It is a mistake, however, to think that every problem presented to a specific leader, in this case the assistant principal, must be resolved by that same leader. Problem solving can also be effectively done by helping the faculty develop strategies that allow them to feel comfortable taking the issue directly to the principal in a way that recognizes how the principal manages information and solves problems.

Understanding this process, the assistant principal can work with and support the teachers so that the issue can be taken directly to the principal in ways that are most likely to be effective. In order to give specific, effective advice to a teacher, the assistant principal needs to have an understanding of how the principal operates and how best to approach the principal. The assistant principal must know how the principal makes decisions and how the principal likes to communicate, and be communicated to, about school issues without feeling defensive or aggressive. In this capacity the assistant principal is serving as a mentor to any faculty who have concerns. The assistant principal is building bridges for effective communication between the faculty and the principal. Since the goal is to fix the problem, facilitating a resolution of the issue so that it can be resolved between the principal and a teacher is an example of a high performing assistant principal in action.

Making Faculty Issues the Assistant Principal's Issues

Often a faculty member will approach the assistant principal with a problem that, in the judgment of the assistant principal, cannot be resolved by advising the faculty member on the best way to approach the principal directly for a resolution. The faculty member involved may not be comfortable in presenting the issue to the principal. There may be ongoing conflict between the principal and the faculty member that will diminish the likelihood for a successful resolution of the problem. In cases like this, an effective strategy for the assistant principal is to see if the issue presented can become an issue not of the faculty member's but of the assistant principal's.

This strategy is particularly effective when the issue can be observed directly by the assistant principal. If the issue is occurring in a public setting such as the classroom or during noninstructional time at school such as during lunch or before school, the assistant principal can observe the problem directly, can pop in on the problem or observe the problem during a walk-through or during campus supervision time, and, thus, can take ownership of the issue. If the issue can't be observed directly but can be seen in the data—for example faculty concerns over the number of students who are tardy to first period or the fact that a particular department feels they are always assigned to teach in portables—or if the issue can, in any way, be discovered independently by the assistant principal through some type of data analysis, then the assistant principal can make the issue an assistant principal issue instead of a faculty issue.

By making the issue one that has been discovered by the assistant principal, the problem becomes not what the assistant principal was told and by whom but what the assistant principal saw or discovered as a natural part of the job's functions and responsibilities. When the assistant principal approaches the principal with the concern, it is the assistant principal's concern that is being brought to the attention of the principal, not the teacher's concern. While the high performing assistant principal should always work to build a school climate in which every teacher and every issue can be vetted in an open and professional manner between faculty members and the principal, it is likely that sooner or later the assistant principal will need to lead faculty members and support principals who are not able to communicate successfully through direct problem solving.

It is important to note that while these strategies are discussed in the context of supporting relationships between the faculty and the principal, it is just as likely, if not more likely, that teachers will seek out the assistant principal not to resolve issues on their behalf with the principal but to resolve issues on their behalf with fellow teachers. Teachers are often reluctant to confront their colleagues regarding behaviors that may be troubling. Perhaps a teacher is concerned about the lack of classroom discipline being maintained by a colleague or feels that certain faculty members are dominating faculty meetings and are misrepresenting the views of the faculty as a whole. In cases like these, the teacher may look to the assistant principal as the individual who can resolve the problem without bringing the teacher directly into conflict with a fellow teacher. The strategies described previously can work to resolve faculty-to-faculty issues in the same manner they can be used to resolve faculty-to-principal issues.

For example, a teacher approaches the assistant principal with complaints about inconsistent enforcement of school-wide rules regarding student hall passes. A colleague is allowing students into the halls to use the restroom or go to their lockers. This behavior is causing student resentment of the concerned teacher, because she is enforcing the rule. By understanding the problem, what it is and when it occurs, it is very easy for the assistant principal to directly observe the questionable behavior and directly approach the colleague in question about the issue without having to ever bring other teachers into the discussion.

Making Consistency, Transparency, and Trust the Hallmarks of Faculty Interaction

Regardless of the circumstances or the issues involved, the cornerstones for all successful relationships in the school setting must be consistency, trust, and transparency (Burke, Sims, Lazzara & Salas, 2007; Tschannen-Moran, 2014). The assistant principal must lead in a manner that is consistent. Faculty need to know that the assistant principal can be counted on, day in and day out, to behave and react in predictable ways, whether the issues of the day involve student interactions or faculty interactions, or when the assistant principal is representing the principal and the school at stakeholder functions. The assistant principal must also lead in a manner that is transparent. The faculty must see that what the assistant principal says is what the assistant principal does. The faculty must be able to see that the assistant principal is working on behalf of them and the students in the school. The faculty must see that the assistant principal's decision-making processes have been developed collaboratively and with consideration for the impacts these decisions may have on the faculty. When the assistant principal is transparent and open with the work being done, positive and professional faculty interactions will follow.

Finally, the assistant principal must lead in ways that build trust with the faculty. Trust is the one prerequisite that must be in place between the faculty and the assistant principal if the assistant principal is going to function as an effective instructional leader within the school. By operating in ways that show transparency to all stakeholders, in both the assistant principal's motives and actions, and by operating with consistency, the assistant principal can begin to build trust with all stakeholders.

DESTROYING FACULTY TRUST

Trust takes time to build. Faculty and other stakeholders typically need to see the attributes discussed here occurring over time before they will truly feel they can trust the assistant principal. Faculty and stakeholders need to see the assistant principal's actions matching the assistant principal's words. Trust requires consistency; transparency; open, two-way communication; and a commitment to the mission and vision of the school that is visible to all. Unfortunately trust that has been built over time can be quickly lost. When it comes to the faculty perception of administrators and maintaining trust between teachers and administrators, there are three deadly enemies to avoid. Nothing will diminish the faculty's trust or lower their respect for the school administration more than inconsistency, isolation (a lack of transparency), and ignorance. When it comes to faculty perceptions regarding the principal and the assistant principal as the administrative team, these three I's kill school climate and any culture of trust and collaboration. When it comes to how the assistant principal and the principal are perceived by the faculty, inconsistency kills, isolation kills, and ignorance kills.

The Inconsistency Trap

Consistency is often defined as always making the same decision, regardless of the circumstances, and as never changing an opinion or course of action. On the surface, making decisions with the goal of having consistent outcomes, regardless of the individual circumstances that make up an issue, may seem to be a worthy goal for school leaders; however, as Ralph Waldo Emerson said, "A foolish consistency is the hobgoblin of little minds, adored by little statesman" (Emerson, 1841). Changing one's mind, or recognizing there may be a better way to move forward with a particular project or a student issue, however, does not mean one is inconsistent any more than being loyal means constantly agreeing with someone on all issues. The inconsistency trap discussed here, the type of inconsistency that damages trust between faculty and administration, has to do with inconsistencies in *how* decisions are being made, not *what* decisions are being made. The consistency that is so important to building trust and understanding between the assistant principal and the faculty, or any stakeholder for that matter, is the consistency of process, not of outcome. Being consistent is of no value if the decisions

made are consistently wrong. Being consistent is of no value if the decisions made don't reflect new insights or possibilities for a better path
forward. Being consistent is of no value if the outcomes from the decisions made are not moving the organization forward. Being consistent is
of no value if the organization places a higher value on always having the
same response to every situation rather than having the correct response
to any specific given situation.

There are many examples where the commitment to assuring consistency in decision outcomes, as opposed to assuring consistency in the
process used to arrive at the decision, has poor results. Zero tolerance
policies that call for a consistent response to every violation of school
drug policies, for example, often escalate the problem in a manner that is
disproportional to the violation itself. When administrators handle students dealing with a minor, first-time offense the same way a student
with a major felony arrest is handled, the claim of consistent outcome can
be made. The more important question should be, can the claim of equitable and just treatment for both students be made in such cases? Should
the student who gives a classmate an aspirin for a headache, in direct
violation of school policy, receive the same consequence as the student
who is arrested on campus distributing felony narcotics? The inconsistency trap that kills trust between faculty and the assistant principal–principal team is not found in the different outcomes as a result of a
particular set of facts or circumstances; it is found when different and
inconsistent processes and procedures are used to arrive at those outcomes.

The fundamental question the administrative team needs to attend to
is, are the agreed on policies, procedures, and school practices for *arriving*
at decisions consistently applied? Are the principal and assistant principal consistent in how they communicate to stakeholders, when they communicate to stakeholders, and with whom they communicate on given
issues? How often do teachers feel the assistant principal and principal
have faculty favorites or an administrative "A" team who are privy to
information that the rest of the faculty do not receive or who are consulted with regarding decisions in a way that is not part of the formal
communication process of the school? It is when this type of inconsistency or lack of transparency in school procedures or in faculty access to
information or decision making that erodes trust between the faculty and
the administration. This approach or process will always result in a perceived or actual lack of transparency between the assistant principal and
the faculty, resulting in the loss of trust between faculty and administration and a sense of unease and uncertainty regarding the decision-making process itself. How the administrative team communicates, with
whom the administrative team communicates, under what circumstances
the administrate team decides to communicate, and whether all these
aspects of the communication process are handled in a transparent and

predictable manner says a great deal about how the assistant principal and principal use their position power within the school.

The assistant principal–principal relationship and how that relationship is perceived by all the school's stakeholders become the administrative brand of the school. Just like there is a Disney brand or a Neiman Marcus brand, there is also branding that occurs in schools regarding the administrative team leading the schools. What that brand becomes—what the assistant principal is known for and what the administrators as a team are known for—is a reflection of who the leaders are, how they behave, and on what they can be counted on to do and be on a consistent and transparent basis.

The Isolation Trap

Get out of the office. The second leadership trap is isolation. It is all too easy and common for the assistant principal to become physically isolated from the faculty and student body by becoming office bound. This author has seen school administrators committed to avoiding the isolation trap go so far as to physically remove their office doors, thus, creating a literal "no door" policy as a way to symbolize an open collegial relationship between themselves and the faculty. Faculty would come and take pictures of the office with no doors. Emails were sent to colleagues in other schools talking about the new "no door" policy at their schools. While the gesture was largely symbolic, it mattered to the teachers. It sent a loud and powerful message that collaboration and open, transparent leadership would be the order of the day. Creating the time to be an instructional leader will be examined in detail in chapter 9. Simply put, however, the effective assistant principal should spend at least 50 percent of the workday involved in leadership activities directly connected to teaching and learning that support the mission of the school. The assistant principal can become consumed by administrative job functions that are necessary for efficient school operations but do not move the school forward in the areas of curriculum, instruction, student achievement, and professional development. Establishing the expectations and ground rules with the principal regarding how a typical day will be spent as a leadership team is a critical task for the assistant principal. Just as the assistant principal must avoid becoming isolated from the faculty, so too must the principal remain visible and accessible to all stakeholders.

It is a common practice for principals to assign management tasks such as student discipline, housing, testing, master schedules, and supervisory responsibilities to the assistant principal so that valuable time can be allocated for the principal, as the instructional leader of the school, to attend to instructional leadership activities. This practice is particularly common in large secondary schools where a team of assistant principals may be assigned to the school, each with a primary job function, such as assistant principal for facilities or assistant principal for student services. This delegation of management functions is appropriate. It makes sense to have a clearly delineated organizational structure so that stakeholders know who to go to for the answer to a question or to get tasks accomplished. It makes sense for the principal to operate within a structure that assures visibility and attentiveness to instructional issues.

This issue of the assistant principal as manager was discussed in chapter 3 in the context of the assistant principal's need to find and maintain not just a management voice but an instructional leadership voice. It doesn't make sense, however, to allow management tasks to overwhelm the workday and, thus, the leadership functions of the assistant principal. Once the assistant principal becomes physically isolated from the principal or the faculty, regardless of the work that may be occurring, the assistant principal loses the ability to lead. For this reason, the assistant principal and principal must establish mutually agreed on goals and behaviors regarding school priorities and how this precious resource of time will be allocated so that no member of the leadership team becomes isolated from leadership work or from the faculty and other stakeholders in the school. It has been the experience of this author that assistant principals who dedicate the majority of their time to managing daily operations and putting out fires do not have the time or the capacity to lead instructionally.

There is a second type of leadership isolation that is harder to see than physical isolation but just as dangerous to the leadership team. Intellectual isolation kills trust and collaboration. Intellectual curiosity and lifelong learning, on the other hand, foster collaboration and quality decision making (Blasé & Blasé, 2000; Hargreaves, 2004). High performing assistant principals are curious about how teaching and learning work. They have an open mind to new ideas and ways of reaching organizational goals. They like to live in solution space, not problem space. When the assistant principal or the administrative team gets locked into thinking that there is just one way to problem solve or one solution for any given problem, however, intellectual isolation occurs. Preconceived notions about particular individuals or groups of stakeholders often reinforce stereotypes and diminish the possibility for collaboration within the entire school structure. When the administrative team is perceived by the faculty to be isolated intellectually, to be rigid in its thinking and actions, the faculty will also become isolated not just from the administrative team but from the stakeholders they serve on a daily basis: the students, the parents, and their colleagues. The high performing assistant principal participates in professional development alongside the faculty. If skill development in classroom management, assessment, or instructional strategies is worth the time of the faculty, then that skill development is worth the time of the school administration. Too often, administrators will coordinate staff development and discuss how important the training is to the mission of the school but then not participate in the process or only introduce the training sessions and then move on to other activities.

The Ignorance Trap

The third principal–assistant principal leadership trap is ignorance. As discussed, effective administrative leadership teams are built on expert power, not position power, and that expert power must be demonstrated by every member of the administrative team. The leadership team does not fall into the ignorance trap when an answer is not known. The ignorance trap occurs when the team does not care about finding out what the answer or best path forward is. Expert power is much more than knowing what to do in any particular set of circumstances; it is about wanting to know what to do. We are not ignorant when we don't know the answer. We are ignorant when we don't care about the answer, when we don't want to learn. Assistant principals who attain their positions having just completed advanced degrees in educational leadership may feel that they are being paid to provide the answers. This is not the case. The assistant principal as instructional leader is being paid to facilitate, motivate, and guide a school community of leaders toward collective and collaborative problem solving. Educators work in learning communities; the schoolhouse is the epicenter of formalized teaching and learning. Assistant principals hold a unique position in the profession and must model lifelong learning and intellectual curiosity. Faculties don't expect assistant principals and principals to have all the answers; they do, however, expect the leadership team to want to find the answers. High performing assistant principals do not rely on position power when an answer or path forward is not known. High performing assistant principals rely instead on expert power, which is much more than knowing what to do; it's knowing how to learn, how to collaborate, and how to problem solve. When the faculty perceive the administrative team as intellectually uninterested in attempting to solve the complex problems at hand, there is no way the faculty will remain intellectually interested in solving the problems at hand. When the assistant principal–principal leadership team models intellectual curiosity and collaboration, the faculty will become motivated and much more likely to be collaborative partners in the problem solving process.

SIX

The Teachers Union: Opportunity or Adversity?

In July of 2011 the team owners of the National Basketball Association (NBA) locked out the players over failure to reach a collective bargaining agreement for sharing league revenue. In short, the owners and players of the NBA stopped working over salary and working condition disputes. At the time of the strike the average salary for an NBA player was 5.15 million dollars a year (Aschburner, 2011), and the net worth of an NBA owner ranged from a high of 17.8 billion dollars to a low of 1.5 billion dollars (Smith, 2014). Yet even with this staggering amount of wealth and resources, there was enough dissatisfaction between the billionaire owners and the millionaire players in the area of wages and working conditions to lead to a work stoppage.

If millionaires and billionaires cannot agree on an equitable distribution of financial resources or contract language regarding working conditions and job expectations, why would we expect teachers to be satisfied with their compensation, number of holidays, or myriad of other issues surrounding working conditions faced by today's educator. It is certainly true that for many school systems in America today, the battle over wages, compensation, and working conditions seems like an annual tradition. The teachers union blames management for not prioritizing wages and benefits. Management responds by saying financial resources are limited, and while every effort is being made to compensate employees, the union just doesn't understand there are many financial obligations that must be met in order to operate the system. The costs for health insurance, electricity, busses, technology infrastructure, building maintenance, student and staff safety, instructional material costs—one could go on and on with this list, which grows faster than any increases in local school budgets.

Often, the principal and assistant principal get caught in the middle. How should the assistant principal, one of the few administrators working with teachers on a daily basis, respond when teacher morale or school climate are being impacted by union-management conflict? This chapter examines the relationship traps assistant principals can fall into with union issues and how to avoid those traps or, better yet, establish a climate that effectively focuses teachers away from job dissatisfaction with wages and conditions and instead on job satisfaction with teaching, learning, and student achievement. We will examine the research regarding teacher job satisfaction and look at concrete steps the assistant principal can take to work with faculty and union leaders to increase job satisfaction. By understanding the desire for "adequate" compensation and equity in the allocation of resources we all share, and learning how to separate those needs from the desire we also all share to positively impact the lives of the children we teach, the assistant principal can create a climate of opportunity, not adversity, with union leaders on the faculty.

FACULTY TRAPS

If the assistant principal is one of the administrators closest to the classroom teacher in terms of daily interaction, it should be no surprise that when contract issues, working condition complaints and, concerns over the implementation of policies or practices occur, the assistant principal will often be involved in some manner. How the assistant principal responds to these issues goes a long way toward determining how the faculty and the administration (principal, district staff) view the assistant principal.

There are several common union issue relationship traps that should, and can, be avoided (see figure 6.1). These traps should be avoided not simply to lessen stress or avoid conflict but rather because these traps weaken the relationships between teachers and administrators. In addition, the solution to these traps positively impact school climate; teacher morale,; the assistant principal's ability to lead; and, most importantly, student achievement.

Trap 1: The Chip on the Shoulder

In 1830 the *Long Island Telegraph* reported on the practice of schoolboys planning to fight over a perceived grievance, showing their determination to be seen as tough by having one protagonist place a chip of wood on their shoulder and dare the foe to knock it off ("Chip on shoulder," 2014). The chip becomes a symbol of a grievance or a wrongdoing of some kind that the wearer is entitled to. The chip has been earned.

Trap One: The chip on the shoulder.

   a.) Be a reflective practitioner.

   b.) Be purposeful about chip removal.

   c.) Pause before reacting when authority is questioned.

Trap Two: Whose side am I on?

Trap Three: I think I know the contract.

   a.) Review any changes in the contract with the principal.

   b.) Meet with faculty union leaders to review contract changes.

   c.) Review contract language prior to making contract related decisions.

   d.) The goal is contract compliance.

Trap Four: It's just about the money

Figure 6.1.   Faculty Traps

It is a simple matter of fact that school assistant principals will always have reasons to place chips on their shoulders. It is inevitable that students, teachers, other administrators, basically any constituency with which an assistant principal works, will behave in ways that make the assistant principal's job more difficult or will result in some form of unfair, unjust treatment of the assistant principal. As a result of these slights, oversights, and often premeditated attacks, assistant principals can gather these chips and place them on their shoulders, often never to be removed but instead carried around like badges of honor, as recognition that the job includes a form of ongoing baptism by fire. While it may feel just and righteous to collect and carry these chips, they are in fact a leadership trap.

The "chip on the shoulder trap" is all too common with principals and assistant principals when dealing with the frustrations of teachers and staff over compensation and working conditions. The author has seen many assistant principals get caught up in the negative energy surrounding contentious union-related issues or, worse yet, strike back in word or deed when treated poorly by faculty over issues that may or may not be beyond the assistant principals' control. The "chip on the shoulder trap" is not, however, confined to dealing with teachers frustrated over union issues or other management issues. The assistant principal can just as easily fall into this trap when working with students, parents, or in any other constituency.

It is human nature to feel bruised, put upon, or treated unfairly whenever someone behaves irrationally or in a way that makes your job more difficult or unpleasant. If this happens often enough when dealing with a particular individual, group, or topic, it is natural for leaders to place those chips on their shoulders and carry them around. The problem with carrying these bruises around is they not only impact how leaders perceive the issues being faced, the ability to lead effectively, they also impact how assistant principals are perceived by others, by the constituency they are working with. If teachers perceive that the assistant principal is hostile to a certain group of colleagues or a certain issue, if they believe the assistant principal is not treating everyone fairly and with dignity and respect—*even if* the assistant principal has not been treated fairly or with dignity and respect—the ability to collaborate, to be effective as a leader will be diminished.

Effective assistant principals develop strategies to take chips off their shoulders. The effective assistant principal consciously removes the chips that have built up from the previous day and removes them so that every day begins "chip free." The effective assistant principal has the ability to have a positive attitude toward people or issues, even when a negative attitude is justified. Anyone can be mad or irritated at someone who has treated him or her poorly. Leaders, however, learn strategies to let go of these grievances, to be proactive and positively oriented with each new day and new challenge.

As an effective assistant principal, you must do the following to take chips off your shoulders:

- *Be a reflective practitioner.* High performing assistant principals have the ability to honestly reflect for a few minutes each day about who and/or what is bothering them. Leader can't take the chips off if they don't know what those chips are.
- *Be purposeful about chip removal.* It's not just actions but also thoughts that influence perceptions of work and the people with whom the work is occurring. Effective leaders begin every day with a positive attitude directed specifically toward the individual, groups, or issues that have been most troubling. Effective leaders make a conscious effort to treat those individuals or events that have proven to be frustrating or unfair to the leader with a fresh start every day. These leaders remove these chips, these grievances—over and over again, if needed.
- *Pause before reacting when authority is questioned.* Modern American schools are open social systems. The power vested to the assistant principal by the authority of the position, commonly referred to as position power, is not a particularly effective tool for moving facul-

ty and staff toward school goals. Teachers and students may comply with directives from administrators, but few teachers are going to go the extra mile just because the assistant principal said to. It is the use of expert power and charismatic power that will motivate stakeholders and move the school forward in a way that maintains a positive school climate and supports a collaborative school culture.

Unfortunately, it is common for one of the biggest chips on a school administrator's shoulder to come from the questioning of that administrator's authority to make a certain decision or act in a certain manner. The administrator may very well have the authority to do exactly what is being directed to employees. In the case of the assistant principal, the principal may have even directed or delegated the assistant principal to take a specific action. When tasks or actions have been delegated to the assistant principal, however, it is not effective to explain that everyone should proceed as directed simply because the assistant principal or principal said so. The effective assistant principal will put position power directives in context, will answer questions about the directive, and will seek feedback about how the directive might be implemented so that everyone impacted feels comfortable with the purpose of the action and feels confident that the steps being taken have been well thought out and are necessary. When leaders take the time to place actions in context and seek feedback about those decisions, the occasions when the use of position power is needed will be received and implemented with more support than that same directive being assigned out of context and with little or no communication.

When decisions and authority are questioned, however, the high performing leader takes a step back to pause and reflect. Unless the issue has to do with student or staff safety or is urgently time sensitive, effective assistant principals fall back on facilitative leadership skills and on expert power. The time a leader takes to discuss and review recommended actions with the individuals questioning the authority or wisdom of those actions will pay dividends many times over when it comes to building a sense of team between the administration and the faculty, rather than building a bureaucracy that separates management from faculty or staff.

Trap 2: "Whose Side Am I On?"

The assistant principal is a leader in the middle of an organization, with the principal as the direct supervisor on one side and the faculty as the primary stakeholder on the other. Chapter 7 examines the many challenges and opportunities that come with leading and impacting teaching and learning from the middle of the organizational flow chart. One potential union pitfall that often arises when leading from the middle is the assistant principal's decision regarding whose side to be on when there is the inevitable conflict between faculty and administration regarding a policy, practice, working condition, or pay dispute. This decision is a leadership trap. The decision regarding whose side to be on, faculty's or management's, assumes a false "either/or" dichotomy. The assistant principal who is rigidly aligned with the position of the principal, regardless of the merit of the faculty position, or supports individual faculty members or subgroups behind the principal's back is doomed to leadership failure with both groups. In fact, the answer to whose side the assistant principal should be on is easy to identify but hard to implement. The assistant principal as an instructional leader and educator should be on the students' side. The good news is, despite all the disagreements the assistant principal will face, all stakeholders are educators and instructional leaders, and they, too, are on the students' side. The high performing assistant principal consciously articulates this viewpoint toward what is best for students over and over. The effective assistant principal uses this viewpoint to redirect conflict away from taking sides between adults and toward siding with what is best for the students in the building. It is common to hear the following at a colleague's retirement: "She always acted with the students' best interest in mind." It is the rare leader, however, who consistently does so.

Trap 3: "I Think I Know the Contract"

All too often conflict arises and mistakes are made because school leaders assume they know the protocols and procedures outlined in the collective bargaining agreements or in school board policy. Not only are contract violations embarrassing for the assistant principal, by not knowing the language in union contracts, the assistant principal is weakened as an authority and an expert. Contract language is always changing. It is not uncommon for subtle changes in timelines, procedures, notification processes, forms, and the like to be made on an annual basis. It is also often the assistant principal who is left out of the teacher contract orientation meetings held by district staff with school principals. Thus, the assistant principal may have no formal induction into contract language amendments. It is also problematic when the perceived intent of contract language is not considered prior to making decisions. Often the language is ambiguous and can be interpreted in different ways depending on the issue. It never hurts to consult with union representatives prior to making decisions, as this enhances collective team spirit.

By following some simple strategies, the assistant principal can go a long way toward assuring actions taken are in compliance with all union contracts:

- *Review any changes in the contract with the principal.* Both the principal and the assistant principal need to make sure they both have the same understanding regarding the contract language and any changes made from the previous year and that any necessary adjustments to school-based policies and procedures as required by the contract have been made. As a team, the assistant principal and the principal should also establish, in advance, the procedures for communicating with each other about .contract concerns that arise from teachers or the administration.

- *Take the time to meet with faculty union leaders to review contract changes.* It is not just the administrative team that needs to have a clear understanding of the contract as each year begins. Faculty union leaders and the faculty as a whole also need to be aware of, and understand, contract amendments. The principal and the assistant principal, as a team, should discuss with the faculty the changes that have occurred and the commitment of the administration, assuring full and transparent compliance with any new contract language. Effective school leaders let the faculty know that they are attentive to the contract, want to abide by the contract language, and look forward to a collaborative implementation of the document. Remember, the contract also calls on specific behaviors, timelines, processes, and procedures from the faculty as well as the administration. The contract can be a very useful tool to assist the assistant principal in working with teachers to accomplish tasks and meet deadlines.

- *When an issue arises that may involve the contract, take the few minutes necessary to review the language in the contract before making an executive decision.* The effective leader wants to get things right. Union leaders and teachers also want decisions made to be contract compliant and appreciate it when school leaders show, through their actions and deliberations, that contract compliance is not a burden but rather an important part of a trusting relationship between teachers and administrators. The time spent to research a contract issue or seek advice from the principal or appropriate district staff before making a decision regarding a contract dispute is time well spent. Everyone involved will be better served by a correct and accurate interpretation of contract language.

- *On those rare occasions when a contract-related mistake is made, remember the contract goals high performing administrators have.* High performing principals and assistant principals want to be in compliance with the contract. When these administrators find themselves out of compliance, they have one goal: get back into compliance as quickly as possible and let the faculty know they are pleased to correct the error. Too often leaders feel defensive or place the chip on their shoulder when an administrative error occurs. These administrators want to defend their original positions or deflect the decision away from themselves. All leaders make mistakes. Effective leaders correct the mistakes they have made as a way to improve their own performance and expertise. Effective leaders see these corrections as an opportunity to serve as a role model for other stakeholders, who will certainly make their own mistakes in the future and need to decide how to respond to those mistakes.

Trap 4: It's Just About the Money

Wages, benefits, and working conditions clearly dominate most union management contract discussions and disputes. Faculty lounge conversations, newspaper reports, union and management written communications, such as newsletters or email updates, can easily give the impression that when it comes to the adults in the building, it's all about the money. The reality, however, is much more complex.

As discussed, the assistant principal has one of the most complex jobs in the organization. The assistant principal is often the first adult in the building each day and the last to leave each evening. An examination of the education required for the job, the degree of responsibility the assistant principal is given, the expectations the assistant principal must achieve, and the tremendous responsibility of caring for and educating the children quickly reveal that today's assistant principal is significantly underpaid and anyone who looks at the typical assistant principal salary versus the job responsibilities will know it. It is a mistake for any educator to calculate their hourly wage based on the actual hours worked. This is true for the superintendent of schools; this is true for the principal and the assistant principal; and it is certainly true for the classroom teacher.

Despite this fact and the legitimate interests in increasing compensation that all educators share, it would be the rare assistant principal or leader who would say that frustration over salary, or other areas of concern regarding working conditions, impacts his ability to either do his job well or his ability to remain committed to the goals and objectives of the organization. The school's principal and assistant principal believe they can, and do, separate money issues from overall job performance. The effective school administrator also recognizes that teachers facing the same salary and working condition frustrations also feel capable of separating money issues from job performance. If the principal and the assistant principal can compartmentalize the issues of wages, benefits, and working conditions from the issues of teaching and learning, so can the faculty and staff. It is a misunderstanding of school climate, culture, and human nature to assign a blanket set of motives to individual teachers or to groups of teachers by saying their behaviors and motivations are "all about the money." The assistant principal who does assign this motivation to her colleagues limits the ability for both she and the teacher to have meaningful dialogue and collaboration around school goals. The assistant principal who recognizes the true motivation of teachers as well as the complexities and nuances of such motives can build opportunities for faculty collaboration despite any ongoing financial battles at work within the building.

RESPONDING TO CONTRACT VIOLATION INQUIRIES

Union management relationships are complex by nature. This complexity does not have to mean that all union–school management relationships must be negative or confrontational. Too often, however, school principals and assistant principals do default to an antagonistic view of the union. This negative attitude toward the union can be exacerbated by the inevitable grievance claim filed by a teacher over a perceived contract violation. As a front-line administrator, it is often the assistant principal who is implementing district or principal policies, practices, and procedures for the daily operations of the school. Inevitably there will be some disagreement regarding the implementation of all of these policies and procedures, and claims will be made that the school administration is violating contract provisions. It is not fun to be accused of violating the teacher contract; it is stressful and can feel like a personal attack. Assistant principals who are accused of a contract violation not only find themselves dealing with the accusation from the teacher; they also must deal effectively with the principal or district administrators who will be inquiring about the actions taken to investigate the facts of the event in question. To complicate matters, on some occasions the assistant principal may have been implementing a procedure or process exactly as directed by the principal. How the assistant principal manages the attitudes and expectations of the principal with issues such as these are critical to his overall success as a leader. In cases involving conflict or disagreement between the assistant principal and a teacher or staff member over a contract issue, as is the case in so many situations faced by today's assistant principal, the assistant principal is working from the middle of the organization, with the faculty on one side and the principal on the other.

How, then, should an assistant principal respond to an allegation of a contract violation by the union? It is important to remember that the contract, and all the language and provisions contained within the contract, have been mutually agreed on. The contract is not just the contract written by the teachers union; it is also the contract written by the administration. The contract was negotiated and agreed to by both parties: the teachers union and the school district. Both parties have agreed, in writing, to abide by the provisions within the contract. Both parties want to abide by the language within the contract, including the effective school administrator.

There are two possible outcomes from any contract dispute: (1) It is found that no violation of the contract occurred. (2) It is determined that a violation of the contract has occurred. If it is determined no violation in substance or principle occurred, this is obviously good news. All the requirements in this mutually written and agreed on document are being met. This is a good opportunity, however, for both the school administration and the faculty involved to gain a further understanding of the language in question and to understand that the school procedures in question are appropriate.

The high performing assistant principal will go a step farther, however by exploring the following questions:

1. What are the underlying frustrations and anxieties that led to the complaint in the first place?
2. Does this complaint represent the concerns of one individual faculty colleague or does it represent an underlying frustration shared by many within the faculty?
3. Even though the action did not violate the contract, is there a better way to deal with the underlying issue in the future?

When teachers see that a finding of no administrative wrongdoing regarding a contract grievance is not a cause for celebration or gloating but instead an opportunity to improve communication, collaboration, and trust, school climate and leadership effectiveness as an assistant principal will only improve. Too often leaders fall into a false win-lose narrative rather than creating win-win narratives when it comes to conflict over union contracts.

As mentioned earlier, the second probable outcome of a union dispute is a finding that a violation of the contract has occurred. Contrary to the reaction of most school leaders, this is also good news. Every effective school leader wants to be in compliance with all state and federal statutes, school board policies, and union contracts. When something isn't working, effective leaders want to fix it. When something can be done better, high performing leaders want to do it better. It is good to find out that a certain policy, procedure, or practice that you have been carrying out is in conflict with the teacher's contract. It is good because the assistant principal and principal are in a position to fix the policy, procedure, or practice in error, and this is what both parties, administration and the teachers in question, want. Outstanding school leaders are not defensive when a possible grievance or inquiry occurs. Outstanding school leaders fix the problem and show they respect the contract and the contract resolution process. Effective assistant principals also remember trap 1 and keep any chip that might have been created through the contract resolution process off of their shoulders.

SALARY, WORKING CONDITIONS, AND JOB SATISFACTION

Frederick Herzberg's motivation-hygiene theory (Herzberg, 1966) regarding what does and does not motivate employees has stood the test of time. His research showed that in the area of wages, compensation, and working conditions, all employees view their jobs on a continuum of "job dissatisfaction" not "job satisfaction." This "dissatisfaction index" ranges from neutral (the best management can hope for) to completely dissatisfied. Nowhere on the index, when it comes to salary, is the employee ever "satisfied." There is always someone making more. There is always some degree of concern that the funds available for salaries are not being used wisely or distributed equitably among employees. This theory on motivation, job satisfaction, and wages can be seen in action with the ubiquitous wage disputes between millionaire and billionaire athletes and owners. The danger school-based administrators face in this endless conflict over salary and working conditions is the tendency to get distracted by these issues or, worse yet, to begin to develop a negative attitude toward the union in general and teacher leaders in the union in particular. It is easy to generalize negative teacher attitudes toward contract negotiations, salaries, and working conditions as representing teacher attitudes toward curriculum, instruction, professional development—in short, their attitudes toward teaching and learning. The bad news is administrators from all levels have a tendency to generalize about teacher union issues in just that way. The good news is teacher job satisfaction can be impacted more by student success than almost any other factor, and school assistant principals can play a key role in developing teacher-administrator relationships focused on teaching and learning as opposed to bus duty assignments or contract language.

TEACHING, LEARNING, STUDENT ACHIEVEMENT, AND JOB SATISFACTION

While it seems there is a constant negative attitude toward salaries and working conditions, the good news is the research doesn't support this generalized view of negative teacher attitude toward students and teaching in general. On the contrary, teachers are able to separate their views on salary and compensation from their views on teaching and learning. The high performing assistant principal needs to be able to do the same. The research suggests that it is not higher salaries that motivate teachers but student success and student achievement (Brunetti, 2001). What moves teacher attitudes from the "dissatisfaction index" to the "satisfaction index"? Student success does. When it comes to helping students learn, teachers' and school administrators' needs are perfectly aligned. Student success is not only the primary mission for both administrators and teachers; it is what provides the most job satisfaction for both teachers and administrators.

The research is clear that teacher job satisfaction is linked directly to student achievement (Blandford, 2000; Nguni, Sleegers, & Denessen, 2006; Cerit, 2009). When teachers are more successful at raising the academic achievement of their students, job satisfaction also rises (Bogler, 2001). When teachers are provided with the knowledge and skills necessary to be successful with their students, job satisfaction rises. It is when the teacher is able to make their own competence impact student learning that job satisfaction is most correlated to student achievement (Caprara, Barbaranelli, Steca, & Malone, 2006). Seeing students learn produces happy teachers. In fact, student achievement is reported as a "very important" factor in the overall job satisfaction of teachers (Brunetti, 2001).

Principals and assistant principals need to recognize that if they are perceived by teachers as only interested in a confrontational relationship with teacher unions, then efforts to engage teachers in meaningful reform designed to improve student achievement will be weakened. Having a positive academic impact on students and being able to use instructional skills to meet students' academic needs can be a primary source for teacher job satisfaction (Plihal, 1982, Nguni et al., 2006). The fact that increasing the performance of students significantly raises the satisfaction of the teacher can be used as a starting point for repositioning both teacher leaders and school administrators to rebuild and reengage in a collaborative approach to increasing teacher effectiveness focused on student learning.

This relationship between job satisfaction and the quality of learning by students is worth repeating. When teachers experience success and competence in the classroom, job satisfaction rises.

The same positive relationship between job satisfaction; educational effectiveness; and meaningful collaboration between teachers, assistant principals, and principals will occur when teachers and administrators engage in a transformational leadership style that emphasizes common goals, open communication and collaborative decision making.

Figure 6.2 lists six steps that can be used by teachers and school administrators to focus on the common goals of teacher job satisfaction and increased student academic achievement.

UNION-ADMINISTRATION ACTION PLAN

Step 1: Begin with the Principal, Begin with the Faculty

Step 1 must include the full support of the principal to engage in a truly collaborative process with the faculty. Just as the assistant principal should work collaboratively with the principal surrounding teacher

Step One: Begin with the principal. Begin with the faculty.

Step Two: Find the common mission.

Step Three: Stay the course.

Step Four: Keep the process transparent.

Step Five: Build capacity among all stakeholders.

Step Six: Repeat; stay the course.

Figure 6.2. Union-Administration Action Plan

contract issues, the assistant principal should also develop a collaborative action plan for faculty engagement on student achievement with the principal. (More discussion on building a coherent and unified vision and action plan with the principal can be found in chapter 1.) Any agreement regarding teacher-administrator collaboration regarding teaching and learning must include the full involvement of the faculty and faculty leaders. This involvement must begin at the planning stages prior to any project implementation. These agreements must be publicly announced and supported by both word and action, even if other labor/management issues become contentious. Both teachers and administrators can publicly agree to disagree on issues of budget allocation, grievance procedures, working conditions, and other standard contract issues while maintaining a common collaborative goal of increasing student achievement and teacher job satisfaction: a common mission that should be shared by all. The assistant principal is in a unique position to facilitate common agreements as well as issues of concern between the faculty and the principal. The commitment to collaborate on issues surrounding teacher effectiveness and student achievement must be demonstrated repeatedly over time and separated from labor-management issues surrounding compensation and working conditions.

Step 2: Find the Common Mission

The second step in this collaborative process requires both parties to identify and agree to the "common mission" that both share. While tension and public disagreement will often arise over collective bargaining issues such as wages, working conditions, and terms of employment, these differences do not need to dominate the narrative between school administrators and school faculty. The collective bargaining process and the natural stresses that the process entails must be separated from other student achievement goals that both parties can agree to and support. Increased student learning can be a common mission for both parties. Increased teacher morale and job satisfaction can be a common mission for both parties.

Step 3: Stay the Course

In any school, implementing systemic change takes time and requires all parties to stay the course, even when key stakeholders are unsure of the wisdom of the path. Faculty will undoubtedly face some opposition from teacher leaders who fear the union is being "managed" by the school administration or that collaboration with the principal and assistant principal will "water down" the ability of the union to negotiate successfully in the future. School administration will also face opposition. Some district staff or some school-based administrative colleagues will feel that the administration is "handing over" decision-making authority to the faculty and once that happens the school will never be able to recover from that "slippery slope." If both the faculty and the administrative team recognize in advance that these types of anxieties are normal and to be expected, they can be weathered and planned for. As time passes, goals and action plans can be developed and implemented by both parties collaboratively, and the fears and anxieties that exist within the organization will subside.

Step 4: Keep the Process Transparent

The faculty leadership team and the administrative leadership team should announce the common mission, build the action plan, and implement the action plan together and in public. Typically, issues involving contract disputes between unions and school administrators are held in isolated settings with very few observers of the process. Each side independently relays information to stakeholders based on their point of view regarding the success of the negotiations. Distrust and misunderstandings become commonplace. The opposite approach to solving the difficult issues of increasing student achievement must be utilized by both parties. The process must be viewed as fair and accessible to all. Faculty meetings, PTA and other parent advisory board meeting, use of video broadcasts, maintaining and publishing agendas and minutes of joint meetings—are all examples of process transparency. All communication to faculty on issues regarding teaching and learning should be jointly issued. All planning should be conducted in public.

Step 5: Build Capacity among All Stakeholders

Both the school administration and the faculty must identify and recognize all the various stakeholders who play a role in the education process and include those stakeholders in all phases of the work. Surveys, newsletters, emails, town hall meetings, and focus groups are some of the specific strategies that can be used to bring stakeholders to the table. Committees and other working groups can be comprised of members jointly selected by the faculty and administration. Teachers need to feel more than communicated with; they need to feel directly connected to the process. This is demonstrated with evidence that the teacher's voice is present in the work and the final product of that work.

Step 6: I Repeat, Stay the Course

Collaborative project design requires collaborative project implementation. The same requirements, demands, and challenges that both parties face in building new ways to support teaching and learning in the classroom will be faced in the implementation of any meaningful project. The stresses of inadequate time and resources (both human and financial) will always impact the relationship between faculty and school administration.

Contract issues, by their very nature, can lead to differences of opinions and public disagreements. Those differences over compensation and working conditions do not need to inevitably lead to differences over how to design, build, and implement a quality framework for teaching and learning in every classroom. How the assistant principal leads from the middle of the organization and approaches these issues will play a major role in determining whether the school climate and culture is focused on "degrees of job dissatisfaction" or "degrees of job satisfaction."

Today's educators find themselves at a fork in the road. Faculty and school administrators who ignore the common ground, the common goals that both teachers and school administrators share, risk mutual irrelevance: fighting the same labor-management war over and over again. Instead, a transformation of the relationship between teachers and school administrators can occur, resulting in increased capacity to provide them with the knowledge and skills they need to raise student achievement in our schools. This is a goal the effective assistant principal can lead to fruition.

III

The Assistant Principal as Instructional Leader

SEVEN

Leading from the Middle

Because of the very nature of the job, the assistant principal works from the middle of the school organizational structure. The assistant principal is certainly not a classroom teacher. In many states the position is not covered by the teacher collective bargaining unit or teacher tenure laws. The assistant principal is also not the administrative leader of the school. The school principal is recognized and tasked with being the instructional and administrative leader in the school (Fullan, 2010). The assistant principal is the administrator in the middle of the organization working between and alongside the school faculty and the school principal. Serving as the assistant principal, the leader in the middle, comes with many challenges but also with many, often overlooked, unique opportunities to impact the school culture and effectiveness.

CLOSER TO THE ACTION

It is a common expression in public education that the classroom is the "front line" of the school. The classroom is where the action is. Most of the formal outcomes, the standard curriculum all students are expected to master, what most citizens think of as school, happen in the classroom. While the impact of the principal as the instructional leader of the school is clearly documented in the literature, it is the quality of the classroom teacher that research identifies as having the single biggest impact on student achievement (Stronge, Ward, Tucker, & Hindman, 2007; Darling-Hammond & Richardson, 2009).

If it is an accepted fact that the teacher, in the classroom, has the greatest impact on student achievement, it is also common for school-based administrators to fall into a common trap: becoming isolated from the classroom. When the principal or assistant principal become office bound or become firefighters spending the day responding to issues, big and small, this prevents them from being in the classroom or in meetings with faculty that are focused on curriculum and instruction. As a result, teachers may all too quickly begin to feel that that school administrators are losing touch with the day-to-day realities of teaching. How often does a frustrated teacher who is not feeling supported say, "The administration has forgotten what it is like to be in the classroom." For many school and district leaders, there is some truth to this idea: that the higher up the organization one goes, the more out of touch and isolated one becomes. While there are certainly many exceptions to this stereotype—leaders at every level who remain visible involved with teachers in classrooms, professional development workshops, and professional learning community activities—too often the responsibilities of school management overwhelm the workday. Suddenly the school principal or district leader is no longer directly involved as an instructional leader in the classroom with the faculty. Often, principals who are working hard to build time into the schedule for direct classroom observations and instructional meetings with teachers will begin to delegate more and more of the school's management tasks to the assistant principal. This delegation of noninstructional responsibilities places even greater pressure on the assistant principal's day. In chapter 9, specific strategies will be shared on this very topic: how to manage and control the school day so that the instructional leadership tasks of the assistant principal are prioritized over the organizational management tasks of the assistant principal.

While leading from the middle makes it harder to control daily events and obligations than leading from the top of the organization, it is in the middle of the organization, between the principal and the faculty, that the assistant principal can be in a unique position to lead and support both the principal and the teachers by working within the classroom, paying attention to the daily interactions between teachers and students. It is here, in the middle of the organization, that the assistant principal can make these daily interactions with students and faculty a leadership priority. The assistant principal is closer to the daily interactions between students and teachers. The assistant principal is often handling initial inquiries or concerns from parents and other stakeholders. The assistant principal is working on a daily basis with school staff and other ancillary personnel. When an assistant principal takes advantage of the positive effects of these high impact interactions and sees them as an opportunity to lead faculty and support and inform the principal regarding the culture and climate of the school, success ensues.

DELEGATION AS OPPORTUNITY

Most job descriptions in education conclude with the ubiquitous job requirement "other duties as assigned." While any number of these "other duties" may be mundane or may add additional stress to the job, the high performing assistant principal does not see tasks that have been delegated by the principal as one more thing to do; the high performing assistant principal sees these delegated tasks and responsibilities as one more opportunity to interact with key stakeholders. When the principal assigns bus or lunchroom supervision to the assistant principal, this can be viewed as busy work with no real capacity as a leadership opportunity, or that same duty can be viewed as an opportunity to get to know students, to see firsthand the student culture within the school. These routine student supervision assignments that every assistant principal encounters as part of the job are actually opportunities for the assistant principal to serve as a role model for students, to interact with students on behalf of the faculty, to solve problems big and small by being where students are. When the principal assigns student testing to the assistant principal, the high performing assistant principal does not see this as more bureaucratic management functions to be completed and checked off the "to do" list; the high performing assistant principal sees this as an opportunity to interact with, and impact, the most important constituencies in the school, the faculty and the students. How the testing plan is developed, which teachers are involved, how the schedule is established and communicated—all of these decisions are an opportunity to influence the instructional effectiveness of the school. How the testing plan is built is also an opportunity to collaborate with faculty leaders, to establish relationships and remain connected to the faculty, to not fall victim to the stereotype of the school administrator who has lost touch or who manages routine tasks in ways that produce routine outcomes. When the principal assigns the management of the PTA or other parent stakeholder groups to the assistant principal job responsibilities, the high performing assistant principal does not see these tasks as one more set of after-hour meetings but rather as an opportunity to understand the concerns and the aspirations of the community and to serve in a leadership manner that supports those aspirations and responds to those concerns. How parents and other external stakeholders view the assistant principal can also be a key component in how the assistant principal is ultimately perceived and evaluated by the principal and the district. Effective administrators do not underestimate the power of public perception to impact current work or future job opportunities. Whether the delegated tasks involve student functions, faculty functions, or external stakeholder functions, delegated tasks are opportunities that high impact assistant principals use to lead.

THE EYES AND EARS OF THE PRINCIPAL

When the assistant principal is working closely with students, teachers, and external stakeholders, this is a significant opportunity to influence and impact the organization directly; it is also an opportunity to serve the principal as an extra set of leadership eyes and ears. Often the problems or issues that may be occurring within the school or the frustrations that may be building with various constituencies may be seen first by the assistant principal who is in a position of visibility to faculty, students, and stakeholders, and has established trust from faculty, students, and stakeholders.

Effective principals want and expect their assistant principals to be another set of eyes and ears for the principal. Effective principals want and expect their assistant principals to understand the culture and climate of the school, to understand what is happening within both the formal and informal communication networks between school stakeholder's and faculty members. No high performing principal will resist or resent an assistant principal who is trying to be more supportive of the mission of the school faculty and principal by staying engaged and informed about the school's culture and climate.

While it may seem obvious that the principal expects the assistant principal to serve as a second set of leadership eyes and ears and to keep the principal informed of rising issues or new opportunities, it is not as obvious, but just as true, that teachers also want and need the assistant principal to serve as another set of eyes and ears on their behalf. Teachers also want the assistant principal to see and understand the issues they are facing. When a teacher is having challenges with students or parents, the teacher wants the assistant principal to see and understand those challenges and to support the teacher with alternative strategies or with support when meeting with the student or parent or when seeking assistance from the principal. Often the assistant principal will be asked by faculty or other stakeholders to be their voice regarding sensitive issues the stakeholders may be having with the principal. As a leader in the middle, the effective assistant principal is often seen as the best person to facilitate the resolution of an issue between the stakeholder and the principal. How these issues are handled, how they are communicated, and how trust is maintained with the constituency involved and the principal become critical components of effective leadership from the middle.

TRUST IN THE MIDDLE

It is hard to overstate the power or importance of trust as a core component of any collaborative relationship (Dirks & Ferrin, 2002; Sharkie, 2009). Just as trust underlies every successful relationship between the assistant principal and the principal, as we discussed in chapter 1, trust is also a foundational component for the relationship between the assistant principal and the school faculty or other school stakeholders (Bird, Wang, Watson, & Murray, 2009). As discussed, the assistant principal as a leader in the middle of the organization has both great opportunities to lead as well as unique leadership challenges, which, if not handled properly, can destroy the trust and transparency that is needed for effective leadership to occur.

How assistant principals communicate as leaders from the middle of the school hierarchy to both the faculty and the principal they serve and how they maintain trust with both teachers and the principal is a challenging but extremely important component for assistant principal effectiveness. How the assistant principal answers questions such as the following will go a long way toward determining whether the assistant principal is functioning as an asset to both the faculty and the principal or is seen as self-serving or ineffective:

1. What issues should the assistant principal handle independently versus by reporting to the principal for direction prior to any action?
2. What information gathered from faculty should be shared with the principal, and how should that information be shared?
3. What obligations does the assistant principal have to maintain confidentiality of faculty concerns?
4. What are the assistant principal's obligations to keep the principal informed regarding the climate and concerns shared by faculty or other stakeholders, particularly those issues and concerns shared in confidence?

How these questions are answered, on a daily basis, by the assistant principal will go a long way toward either establishing trust with all stakeholders, serving effectively both the principal and the faculty, or establishing the assistant principal as ineffective or untrustworthy. Effective assistant principals must establish and maintain trust with the principal and with the faculty. The assistant principal does not want to undercut the principal by trying to befriend the faculty or by aligning with the faculty in a way that is counterproductive to the work of the principal. Principals don't like surprises. Principals need to be able to trust the assistant principal to provide them with all the information necessary to make the best decisions possible. The quickest way to destroy the principal–assistant principal relationship is to lose trust.

COMMUNICATION, CONSISTENCY, AND TRANSPARENCY FROM THE MIDDLE

Trust is built on effective communication, consistent action, and transparency of both motive and process. How to manage leading from the middle of the school in a way that provides both the principal and the faculty, or other stakeholders, a sense of trust involves how communication is handled by the assistant principal, whether or not the motives and actions of the assistant principal are transparent to everyone involved, and whether there is a consistency of word and action in how the assistant principal responds to issues and people.

Let's begin with communication skills. How communication is going to occur with the principal, under what circumstances the assistant principal will react unilaterally and then report to the principal after the fact, and under what circumstances the assistant principle will seek guidance and direction from the principal prior to any action must be worked out with the principal in advance. Effective communication is skill based but also requires planning (McEwan, 2003; Graham-Clay, 2005). Too often, this critical attribute of team effectiveness and coherence, the plan for how to communicate with each other is taken for granted, resulting in confusion and miscommunication. The assistant principal needs to establish what is nonnegotiable from the principal's perspective regarding communicating about faculty concerns and issues. The assistant principal needs to know that the principal will not betray information shared in confidence, thus, undercutting the assistant principal's credibility with the faculty. What the expectations are regarding the assistant principal as a voice or conduit for faculty concerns or as the eyes and ears of the principal must be worked out as part of the building of the principal–assistant principal leadership relationship. All of these attributes for communication with the principal—planning for effective communication in advance, establishing communication nonnegotiables, and establishing expectations for communication—are also the building blocks for effective communication with the faculty and other stakeholders. The good news is the strategies and skills for effective communication are the same whether the communication is with a student, a parent, a teacher, or the principal.

Another important attribute of all successful communication is consistency, not only of process as just discussed but also of message. The effective assistant principal is not saying one thing to the principal and another to the faculty. If what is being communicated about the same topic changes from one constituent to the next, it is only a matter of time before those inconsistencies are revealed and trust is lost. Even though some decisions or some messages will be more difficult for one stakeholder to hear and accept than another stakeholder, it is critical that information being shared about a specific issue with one stakeholder is the same information being shared with another stakeholder. When the assistant principal in charge of facilities tells the science department the good news that they will be moved from the portables into the main building because they will be closer to the labs and the English department will be moving to the portables, the assistant principal shouldn't then tell the English department that the bad news about the move into the portables was the result of a decision by the principal or the district office, thus, appearing to not support the decisions being implemented.

Finally, effective communication is also accurate communication. It is a trap to pretend to know something that is, in fact, not known. Whether the constituent is a student or the superintendent of schools, effective assistant principals do not communicate rumor or opinion as fact. Effective assistant principals do not make up answers to questions based on what they think the correct answer or information might be. As discussed in chapter 4, expert power is not about knowing all things. Effective communication is not about knowing all things either.

The assistant principal does not want to undercut the faculty and lose the trust of teachers by reporting every confidence directly to the principal when the teacher believes that reporting will not occur. Nothing stops open communication like a lack of trust or transparency. Just as the assistant principal needs to know that confidences will not be compromised, so do teachers. When teachers know in advance that the information they are sharing with the assistant principal is going to be discussed with the principal as one way of finding solutions to issues or alternate paths the school may wish to take, trust and open dialogue can be maintained. Both parties understand the purpose of the communication and the pathways that communication will follow for future discussion and dialogue. However, when teachers believe the communication is confidential and the assistant principal breaks that confidence, open dialogue will stop. Trust will only be maintained when the rules for communication are known and are transparent to all concerned parties. When everyone understands that what is being discussed will be part of the public dialogue, trusting relationships can be maintained. When everyone understands that what is being discussed is confidential and that confidentiality is maintained on a consistent basis, then trusting relationships can be maintained. It is when there is inconsistency in how communication is handled by the assistant principal toward either the principal or the faculty that trusting relationships break down.

COMMUNICATION AND CONFIDENTIALITY

The assistant principal has five basic approaches regarding confidential communication from the faculty or other stakeholders.

More specifically, as noted in figure 7.1, the assistant principle should do the following:

1. Handle the communication about and issues and opportunities presented by the information in a way that absolutely maintains the confidence of the faculty but is still true to the understanding the assistant principal has with the principal regarding such issues.

2. Tell the faculty involved in advance that the communication you are about to have will not be confidential due to the nature of the issue and your previously established obligations to the principal.

3. Share the information with the principal in a way designed to keep the faculty member from ever knowing that the information shared with you in confidence has been shared. This is obviously a dangerous path that puts faculty trust at great risk, and correctly so. While this pathway maintains trust with the principal and keeps the principal fully informed, it can easily lead to breaking the trust of the other party involved.

4. There is a strategy the assistant principal can use when faced with the need to both share the information with the principal and maintain the confidence of the provider of that information. If the principal is secure enough as a leader and recognizes the need for, and value of, the assistant principal maintaining trust with stake-holders, the information can be shared with the principal with the understanding that the source of the information will not be shared. This approach will only be effective if the information itself is not identifiable with any one individual. For example, if the information is specific to the art program and there is only one art teacher in the school, the confidentiality of the art teacher, who gave the information in confidence, is compromised. If, however, the issue involves a primary grade teacher or a member of the

1.) Maintain complete confidentiality of information and source
    a. As pre-agreed upon with the principal
    b. As prescribed by statute and professional codes of ethics

2.) Share with faculty in advance the intent to share information and source with the principal

3.) Share information and source with the principal without notifying faculty of intent to do so

4.) Share information only (source remains anonymous) with the principal

5.) Share information with the principal with the assistant principal as the source

Figure 7.1. Communication and Confidentiality Options

math department, the issue can be presented as a faculty issue while still maintaining confidentiality, due to the larger number of potential teachers represented by the complaint or concern.

5. The effective assistant principal can act as the source of the information. This allows the assistant principle to communicate all the information the principal needs to know and would expect while still maintaining the confidence of the provider. For example, if the art teacher shared with the assistant principal that a group of parents were planning to complain to the school district that the principal was not providing the art program with sufficient art supplies, the assistant principal could communicate independently with those parents to see how they were feeling about the art program. If a parent shares their concern with the assistant principal, it is now the assistant principal who is bringing the concern and information to the principal, not the art teacher.

Assistant principals who are functioning as instructional leaders have a unique opportunity to both understand the climate and culture of the school and to impact the climate and culture of the school. That impact can occur because the assistant principal is able to facilitate the mission of the school by influencing faculty decisions and behaviors. That impact can also occur because the assistant principal is able to facilitate the mission of the school by influencing principal decisions and behaviors. This ability to "lead up" by influencing the decisions of the principal and district administrators will be discussed further in chapter 8. The very challenges that come from leading from the middle of an organization—how to build time into the schedule to remain visible and active with instruction and curriculum; how to build trust, consistency, transparency, and effective communication with all stakeholders—are also the greatest strengths and opportunities that are available to assistant principals, because they are leading from the middle of the organization.

EIGHT

Leading Up: Building Commitment and Support from Your Superiors

There are many significant differences between the administrator who manages a school and the administrator who serves as an instructional leader for the school. These differences are well documented in the literature (Rost, 1998; Ashkanasy & Tse, 2000). One significant difference, however, between a manager and a leader that has not received significant attention involves the direction, or orientation, of the leader's work. This is particularly relevant to the role of the assistant principal as a leader who is operating from the middle of the school organizational structure. For most leaders, work orientation is typically directed down the organizational structure. In this orientation, the leader leads subordinates toward organizational goals and receives direction about the organization's goals from superiors. There is another leadership orientation, however, that can have a powerful impact on the organization and that the high performing assistant principal is in a unique position to provide. That impact occurs when the assistant principal sees leadership orientation as not just focused on those reporting to the assistant principal but also focused up the organization toward the principal and other educators the assistant principal is reporting to. High performing leaders see leading up the organizational structure as just as important and achievable as leading down the organizational structure. This ability to lead up is common with all great leaders, regardless of their position in the organization. Great teacher-leaders impact school-based administrators. Great assistant principals impact the principal they work for. Great principals impact district leaders, and so on.

LEADERSHIP ORIENTATION

The expressions, "That decision does not reside at my pay grade," or, "I'm not responsible for making those kinds of decisions," are examples of leaders who have a leading-down orientation toward their work and their responsibilities as a leader within the organization. These leaders may very well be skilled in communication, expert power, organizational theory, and passion for the work. These leaders may be very effective in influencing the behaviors and attitudes of those members of the organization who report to them. This need and ability to influence others is not limited, however, to those colleagues within the school who report to the assistant principal or to whom the assistant principal has some degree of position power advantage. The ability to influence others is a major component of effective leadership (Pink, 2014). The ability to influence others both below *and* above you is a major component of the high performing leader. Put another way, effective leaders impact those who report to them, outstanding leaders also impact those to whom they report.

STRATEGIES THAT IMPACT

Truly high performing assistant principals, or leaders at any level within the organization, do not see themselves as limited in their ability to only influence subordinates within the organization. The high performing assistant principal sees the primary objective and obligation of the position as the need to lead up the organizational flow chart as well as down the organizational flowchart. The assistant principal's largest impact on the mission and success of the school will not come from completing a "to do" list created by others; it will come from creating a "to do" list that is valued and implemented by superiors within the organizational framework. Highly effective assistant principals are productive at *creating* the vision and the mission for the workplace, not just *implementing* them. Highly effective assistant principals are proactive in their efforts to influence the behaviors and goals of the educators who reside up the organizational food chain. The biggest opportunity to impact the organization can be built into the daily work of the assistant principal by implementing strategies that influence and impact all stakeholders. This impact can be built by modeling excellence; it can be built around the teacher evaluation systems that every assistant principal must attend to, regardless of the other job functions held. Figure 8.1 outlines five specific strategies for the assistant principal to use in order to impact educators to whom the assistant principal reports.

This impact up the organization can be built by establishing networks with other high performing assistant principals. And, finally, this ability to lead up the organization can be built by creating your own job descrip-

1.) Lead Up by Modeling
   a. Model with a Unique Leadership Voice
   b. Model the Vision and Mission of the School
   c. Model with Collaboration
   d. Model with Life-long Learning

2.) Lead Up from the Foundation Given
   a. Grow the Impact of Routine Job Assignments by
       i. connecting assignment to teaching and learning
       ii. using assignments to build collaboration with stakeholders
       iii. developing improved alternatives to assignments

3.) Lead Up through Teacher Evaluations
   a. Become an Expert in the System's Instructional Framework
   b. Use Teacher Evaluations to Network and Collaborate
   c. Connect Teacher Evaluation to Teacher Professional Development
   d. Use Teacher evaluations to bring Actionable Student Data to Teachers
   e. Use Teacher Evaluations to Shift from Management Roles to Leadership Roles

4.) Lead Up by Networking
   a. Join Formal Networks
       i. Job-Alike Networks
       ii. Interdisciplinary networks
   b. Build New Networks
   c. Participate in Informal Networks
       i. Internal Constituent Networks
       ii. External Stakeholder Networks

5.) Lead Up with Unique "To Do" Lists
   a. Develop Self Assigned Projects
   b. Expand on Projects Assigned by Superiors
   c. Develop Project Proposals for Superiors
   d. Seek Mentoring and Feedback

Figure 8.1.   "Leading Up" Strategies

tion as opposed to simply fulfilling a job description created by someone else.

Leading Up By Modeling

Assistant principals, by the very nature of the job, are members of a leadership team. The assistant principal must represent the principal of the school and reflect the values and organizational aspirations of the principal. Assistant principals, however, also need to work from an internal foundation of values and leadership principles that are unique to them. It may be a trite expression, but leaders must be true to themselves in order to be effective. In chapter 3, the need for every leader to find and keep a unique leadership voice and the strategies needed to maintain

those unique leadership characteristics while maintaining team relationships and trust with the school principal were addressed.

Effective leaders are able to align the specific objectives and activities
assigned by others with a leadership voice that is their own. It is true that
high performing leaders often have common skill sets and attitudes toward the nature of leadership. These leaders have a passion for the work;
they seek to accomplish something bigger than themselves in their work;
and they are lifelong learners who are committed to becoming experts in
their chosen fields. These leaders seek collaboration over isolation; they
work on behalf of others rather than for personal gain.

Effective leaders, however, are not clones of each other. The assistant
principal can lead up and influence superiors within the organization by
modeling a unique leadership voice. This voice can be built by observing
the leadership strategies of others who are effective in different settings.
This voice can be built by asking the principal to serve as a mentor for
communication strategies, decision-making strategies, and instructional
leadership strategies. This voice can be built by then taking those strategies and incorporating them into a personal way of leading. This voice
can be built by maintaining a scholarly interest in the field of educational
leadership. Finally, and most importantly, this leadership voice can impact superiors within the organization by modeling both the strategies
for successful leadership and the personal attributes of successful leadership, on a consistent basis.

Every assistant principal should feel comfortable and capable of leading a school in the principal's absence. Every principal should also feel
comfortable that the assistant principal assigned to them has that capabil-
ity to lead. If the principal can't leave the campus and have full trust and
faith in the capacity of the assistant principal to run the school, then the
assistant principal has not been developed to their potential, and the
principal has not met the obligation to serve as the professional development leader of the team.

Leading Up from the Foundation You Are Given

One of the many challenges the twenty-first-century assistant principal faces is the wide variety of job descriptions and duties inherent in the
job. In small schools, the assistant principal may be a generalist involved
in a wide variety of both managerial and instructional responsibilities. In
large schools, the duties and responsibilities for the assistant principal
may be departmentalized. There may be an assistant principal for curriculum, an assistant principal for facilities and schedules, and an assistant
principal for discipline and testing. Regardless of the size of the school or
the number of assistant principals on the job, these job responsibilities
may change with the arrival of a new principal or with turnover within
the assistant principal team at the school. These job responsibilities and

the degree of independence afforded to the assistant principal can also vary depending on the management and leadership style of the principal.

Some principals like to help develop talented leaders. These principals see one of their leadership responsibilities as mentoring other leaders. Other principals tend to maintain a more hierarchical leadership and organizational view of the role of the principal. They are not adept at delegating responsibility and authority; they want to keep decision making centralized and the lines of communication flowing primarily out of the principal's office. Some principals may feel threatened by new project ideas that originate with the assistant principal or by successful implementations of projects led by the office of the assistant principal rather than their own office.

Whatever the assistant principal job responsibilities might be, however, and whatever management style the principal may have with respect to the role of the assistant principal, there is always an opportunity for the high performing assistant principal to influence the impact of the roles assigned. For example, when the principal delegates the job of building the master schedule to the assistant principal, there is an opportunity to use that job responsibility to lead up the organization. The effective assistant principal will not just automatically repeat the schedule that was in place last year. The assistant principal who wants to lead up and influence future practices researches and thinks about ways to improve the schedule in order to meet the needs of students and faculty. The assistant principal can use this assignment to ask any number of questions in an effort to take this current job responsibility of building the master schedule and improving it. Can the schedule be designed to provide more efficiency within the limitations of the facility? Are there ways to build the schedule that will allow for more input and buy-in from faculty? Can the schedule be redesigned so that students needing acceleration or remediation can be served more effectively? The high performing assistant principal does not need to be assigned the task of developing a better educational schedule for students and teachers in order to deliver a better schedule to students and teachers.

Taking the leadership tasks assigned by the principal, no matter how mundane they may be, and creating new insights, new and better ways of achieving the mission of the school—this is leading up the organization. When the assistant principal builds on the foundation of the assigned jobs, there will typically be a corresponding increase in commitment and support from the principal's office and the district office. This increase in awareness and support will occur as a direct result of the innovation and excellence of the assistant principal's work.

While it is certainly desirable to be assigned a significant role in leadership and innovation by the principal as part of a true leadership team, and while having those significant leadership roles will allow the assistant principal to more easily influence decision makers up the organizational ladder, it is not necessary to have those significant instructional leadership assignments in order to influence and lead your superior toward a better way of providing quality teaching and learning.

Leading Up through Teacher Evaluations

Perhaps one of the most fundamental changes impacting school leaders today is the sea change in both the procedures and expectations for teacher evaluations (Darling-Hammond, Amrein-Beardsley, Haertel, & Rothstein, 2012). New assessment systems based on instructional frameworks developed by Charlotte Danielson, Robert Marzano, and others require all school administrators evaluating teachers to have a complete command of the instructional strategies expected of the teacher and the underlying research that supports those strategies. Today's evaluation systems are both controversial and high stakes (Conley & Glasman, 2008). In many states, teacher retention and compensation are tied directly to teacher evaluations. The amount of time required for the school administrator to complete the multiple preconferences, evaluations, postconferences, informal classroom walkthroughs, and the development of professional growth plans with the teachers assigned to be evaluated makes it virtually impossible for any single administrator to handle teacher evaluations for the entire school faculty. The days of the principal handling all teacher evaluations are over for all but the smallest schools. The days of the teacher evaluation cycle consisting of a cursory observation with a brief meeting to sign evaluation forms are over.

Today's assistant principals will evaluate teacher quality and effectiveness as part of their job description. In order to complete this most important assignment, they must be instructional leaders, regardless of the other duties outlined in the job description. In schools with multiple assistant principals, every assistant principal must be an instructional leader. The assistant principal for discipline is actually the assistant principal for discipline and teacher quality. The assistant principal for facilities and the master schedule is actually the assistant principal for facilities, the master schedule, and teacher quality. It is the rare school that has an assistant principal who is not involved in teacher evaluation. Every assistant principal must understand the instructional frameworks that underlie the teacher evaluation system in the district (Peterson, 2004). All administrators in the school will have a caseload of teachers they are responsible for observing and evaluating. This responsibility is at the heart of instructional leadership (Tucker & Stronge, 2005). This responsibility is also an opportunity to lead in the areas of curriculum and instruction, regardless of the other primary job responsibilities assigned.

For example, when a teacher on the assistant principal's list to be evaluated shows the need to be more data driven in their instruction, the assistant principal can begin working with that teacher, as part of the response to the evaluation findings. The assistant principal will need to learn how to use data to inform instruction, as well as how to differentiate instruction based on the data. The assistant principal and teacher can collaborate and learn how to use data as a formative, diagnostic tool. This professional development process allows the teacher to improve his practice and allows the assistant principal to be an instructional leader while still working specifically within the job duties assigned. This type of instructional leadership can be done by the assistant principal regardless of the management style of the principal or the other job responsibilities assigned by the principal. If the assistant principal has even one teacher she is responsible for evaluating, then she has the opportunity, and the responsibility, to be an instructional leader and influence the organization as a whole. The assistant principal should see teacher evaluation as the opportunity to use expert power to impact teaching and learning. The assistant principal should see teacher evaluation as the pathway to influencing the behaviors and practices of superiors and as a way to build faculty trust and commitment.

Schools are open social systems. The teachers the assistant principal is observing and evaluating will share with colleagues the collaboration occurring between the teacher and the assistant principal as part of the evaluation process. Success is a motivator. Teachers want to make a difference in the lives of their students and are happiest when their students are academically sound (Brunetti, 2001). It is a natural occurrence for the teachers the assistant principal is working with to begin talking to each other. Soon there are requests from more teachers at the school, who may be assigned to other assistant principals or the principal, for data meetings because of the success they are hearing regarding this new approach to data-driven instruction.

In this example, the assistant principal worked within the responsibilities given (evaluating the teacher) and built a better instructional system for the teacher to use in the classroom. The assistant principal impacted teaching and learning. That impact is an opportunity to lead up the organization and influence the practices of the principal and other educators not directly assigned to the assistant principal.

Leading Up by Networking

As open social systems, schools consist of both formal and informal networks and structures. They are impacted by a remarkable number of internal and external stakeholders. Despite all of these networks and stakeholders, from students to parents to business leaders to policymakers at every level of government, schools can also, paradoxically, be very isolating organizations. Teachers can find themselves consumed by their own responsibilities in their classrooms and never truly collaborate with other teachers, even those in the same building. This same type of isolation can easily occur with school leaders. Assistant principals are particularly vulnerable to the isolating side effect of the work and are often more likely to work in an environment of isolation from their peers than even the principal. The principal is often connected at some formal level within the organization to the district office. Monthly principal meetings or other district committee assignments are a common component of the school principal's schedule. It is, in fact, often the assistant principal who remains at school to manage the campus in the principal's absence. The assistant principal may find no formal organizational structure designed to build partnerships and collaboration with other assistant principals in the district. Even the critically important work of providing professional development to school leaders is often directed primarily at the principal. After all, the principal is viewed as the instructional leader of the school, not the assistant principal. Common models for providing professional development have school principals receiving training, information, and the opportunity for professional discussion directly with district staff and other stakeholders. This information and training is then typically "handed down" to the assistant principal at the school level by the principal. The quality and timeliness of that communication will certainly vary from principal to principal. This author has worked with many assistant principals who were shockingly unaware of many of the significant issues, strategic plans, and current statuses of the school systems in which they were working. The scarcity of structure and opportunity within school districts for communication among assistant principals partially explains why this type of leadership isolation occurs. There are, however, opportunities for proactive assistant principals to connect and network with other educators in both formal and informal settings.

Building Formal Networks

Formal networks exist in great abundance in today's twenty-first-century school system. Many educators would say that there are so many committees and meetings occurring during the typical work week that there is not sufficient time for teachers and administrators to plan for instruction or assess the quality of teaching and learning that is occurring in the classroom. School districts have curriculum committees, extracurricular committees, and a wide variety of parent and business leader committees. There are committees to develop budgets, review facility plans, negotiate with various unions, adopt textbooks and other instructional materials, hire staff at all levels of the organization, build district calendars—the list goes on and on. While these committees can impact the time assistant principals have available each day, each of these committees also provides an opportunity for the assistant principal to network with other educators and stakeholders impacted by the decisions being made by educational leaders. Often these committees are searching for representation from school leaders. Often these committees struggle to find active, engaged members; after all, everyone is busy with an ever-increasing set of demands and expectations within their own jobs. For most assistant principals, it is easier to not engage. These committee assignments are often not in the assistant principal's job description. It is too time consuming to network, and, after all, networking or serving on committees is not typically done in place of other job duties; these are done in addition to other job duties.

Taking the time to participate in these networking opportunities, however, provides a critical opportunity for assistant principals to impact their profession. Engaging in work outside the school not only provides an opportunity to grow professionally through networking and learning more about the systems in the district and the people who are also active within those systems but also allows other leaders to see the assistant principal working effectively, and with a purpose, on projects not normally connected to the assistant principal's daily responsibilities. For the assistant principal who seeks new opportunities to lead and continue her career within the organization as a principal or district leader in the future, the opportunity to show leadership skills in new settings is expanded by this type of networking. A further examination of opportunities and leadership behaviors for the assistant principal who wishes to pursue the job of school principal can be found in chapter 14, "Pursuing the Principalship."

Building Informal Networks

In addition to the many formal networks in place in today's school system, every educator is also connected to multiple informal networks. The conversations taking place in the hallway, the parking lot, and the faculty mailroom on a daily basis are, in fact, informal networks in action. What the assistant principal says, what the body language of the assistant principal is, who is being talked to, and who isn't being talked to are establishing informal network perceptions, both good and bad. This even occurs outside the school building. Discussions and pleasantries with parents in the grocery store line or being seen at the movie theater are informal networking moments for assistant principals that influence, one way or another, the perceptions of all parties involved.

Recognizing that these daily informal interactions are connected to the overall impressions being sent and received by the assistant principal, and then being able to reflect on those perceptions, is an important part of effective leadership. Informal networks do not have to be limited, however, to a series of random meetings and conversations. Informal networks can also be built and used to grow professionally and impact the larger organization in a positive way (Mulford, 2003).

The Assistant Principal Network

Perhaps the most common naturally occurring informal network is the network built with other assistant principals. There are more assistant principals in the standard school district than any other group of administrators. There are more assistant principals than there are principals or district supervisors. The large number of colleagues working at the same level of the organization provides a wonderful opportunity for assistant principals to network. The wide variety of job assignments being completed by assistant principals and the variety of principal leadership styles provide a wonderful opportunity to learn new skills and leadership strategies. High performing assistant principals network with their colleagues. They have a list of assistant principals they call when they need advice or information. They establish times to get together simply to touch base and share the successes and challenges they faced on a daily basis. They look to network with new colleagues that they don't yet know in order to provide support and seek out new opportunities to learn. These assistant principals see their colleagues as a resource, not as competition.

The Interdisciplinary Network

Perhaps less common than the network of peers, but providing just as powerful an opportunity to grow and impact others, is the interdisciplinary network of colleagues who hold different positions in education or who are external stakeholders with an interest in education. While the job-alike network provides an opportunity to build horizontal partnerships within the organization, interdisciplinary networks provide an opportunity to grow and influence the organization vertically. Effective assistant principals network with teachers, support staff, and parent leaders as well as with principals and district administrators. If the assistant principal is leading from the middle of the organization, the value of establishing relationships and learning from educators who are reporting to the assistant principal and to whom the assistant principal is reporting cannot be overstated. These networks help build and maintain trust as well as expert power. These networks connect the assistant principal to a wealth of expertise that might otherwise be left untapped. These networks are critical for impacting and influencing other educators throughout the system. The high performing assistant principal is engaged and proactive with all the stakeholders within the organization, regardless of their place on the human resources flowchart or any formal organizational obligation to those individuals.

Leading Up by Creating a Unique "To Do" List

Every job description has a list of requirements and expectations, a list of written job responsibilities. The typical assistant principal job description is no expectation. It is common, if not ubiquitous, to see the generic "other duties as assigned" on these lists. Who is assigning these "other" duties? The boss. In short, the assistant principal should be prepared to receive additional relevant job responsibilities not on the official list, and those assignments will come from the principal or other superiors within the system.

What happens, however, when the assistant principal also creates new "other" duties? What happens when the assistant principal develops and proposes additional job duties or responsibilities not only for themselves but also for educators up the organization such as the principal and the school leadership team as a whole? Can assistant principals leverage their creation of new "to do" lists as a way to grow professionally and impact the larger system in a positive way? The answer to that question is a resounding yes; however, how those new duties are developed, communicated, and implemented are critical to the overall success of this strategy.

For example, it is important for the assistant principal to communicate with the principal and every other stakeholder who might be impacted by these suggested new goals and tasks prior to beginning those new tasks. It is important to seek feedback and secure buy-in for these new responsibilities. To be effective, agreements with colleagues to collaborate and support the work being self-assigned or recommended to superiors or colleagues should occur prior to beginning the work, not after. To begin a self-created job assignment unilaterally is to invite a feeling of secrecy or of stepping on others' toes. It is both human nature and organizational nature for each leader to assume a particular role within the organization. When leaders step out of those roles, anxiety, mistrust, or jealousy can be a side effect. Communicating in advance both the nature and the purpose of the new responsibilities and work being undertaken with everyone impacted will not only calm those fears but will also help build support, or at least neutrality. Despite the risk of unsettling the status quo with new initiatives coming from unexpected places, the benefits of having a vision that improves the school and then acting as a leader to bring that vision to reality far outweigh the challenges or risks. In fact, moving the organization beyond what is expected is what impactful leaders do. Impactful leaders don't just complete the work assigned to them; they create new work that supports the mission of the school. High performing assistant principals are proactive not just in how they accomplish their tasks but also in how they develop new tasks to be accomplished. High performing assistant principals have a two-way leadership orientation.

NINE

The 50 Percent Rule

One of the biggest challenge facing instructional leaders is not the quality of the students in the school, the quality of the faculty, the engagement of the parents, or lack of support from central administration. It is time (Aronson, Zimmerman & Carlos, 1999; Farbman & Kaplan, 2005; Dobbie & Fryer, 2011). Time, in many ways, for all educators, including the assistant principal is not a fixed resource; it is a diminishing resource. Even during years when school budgets increased or when there were fewer such as testing, the lack of time in the standard 180-day school year and the six- or seven-hour school day has impacted the ability of educators to accomplish all that is hoped for. As school budgets shrink and student and teacher accountability increase, the number of administrative and support staff available to run the twenty-first-century school is smaller than ever before. While the number of administrators assigned to schools declines, unfunded regulations from local, state, and federal policymakers continue to increase, and the expectations from parents, external stakeholders, teachers, and the students themselves also rise with each passing year (Gratz, 2000; Reynolds, Stewart, MacDonald, & Sischo, 2006; Goyette, 2008; Reynolds & Burge, 2008).

Health and safety concerns within the school building, from the nutritional quality of the food being served in the cafeteria to the safety of the playground, from student bullies or external threats to expectations for accelerated student academic achievement—are all also on the rise (Sprague, et al., 2001; Brown & Munn, 2008). Just the issue of standardized testing often has entire central office departments dedicated to managing test and measurement operations. Local schools, however, often attempt to manage testing and accountability with existing secretarial and administrative staff as well as perhaps a faculty member receiving a small stipend to manage testing. The rapid rise in the number of high stakes standardized tests administered to students throughout the K–12 system have a profound impact on all school stakeholders and leaders (Hursh, 2005; Solley, 2007).

PRIORITIZING TIME FOR LEADERSHIP

Parent expectations regarding immediate feedback and instant communication are also on the rise (Davies, 2005; Goyette, 2008). Today's technology only raises the expectation for communication to be immediate. With cell phones, texting, and other forms of social media readily available and in the hands of many students, what transpires at school can be communicated from the student to home faster than ever before. That communication is often skewed by the student's perspective. There are documented cases of students being sent to the office for a disciplinary infraction and the parent arriving at the school, based on a text from a classmate, before the administrator has had a chance to investigate, much less respond to, the incident. A problem on a school bus may be called or texted in to parents before the bus has arrived back at school and the driver has written an incident report. YouTube videos can be posted and shared with local media regarding a lunchroom altercation, which may result in the need to respond in real time to an issue that ten years ago might have been investigated over a period of days before reaching a conclusion and communicating the event to stakeholders accurately and completely. In the 1970s and 1980s if the assistant principal responded to all phone calls, requests for meetings, and other requests for communication with a stakeholder within twenty-four hours of the request, most educational leaders would consider the assistant principal as being timely and proactive. The twenty-four-hour rule for getting back parents who called or sent in a note requesting a meeting would serve the school leader well. Today, with email, texting, and cell phones, for many parents and community members, twenty-four hours seems like a lifetime. The parent may feel that a communication at 10:15 on a Monday morning requires a response by 11:00 that morning. How many administrators have experienced or heard about the third or fourth call into the office to speak about an "emergency," only to discover that those calls or email requests occurred over a one- or two-hour period and the "emergency" was, in fact, a routine request to discuss a particular issue. School principals, support staff, and teachers may also find themselves operating under this same "hyper" time frame where everything seems to be happening now, everything is urgent, and every issue should be responded to immediately. When this happens to a school leader, when every issue is a priority issue, the administrator falls into the trap of actually having no priorities at all. The effective school leader recognizes the difference between short-term projects and long-term projects. The effective leaders recognizes the difference between an emergency that must be handled immediately, a high priority item that should be handled in the next day or so, priority items that should be attended to over the next few weeks, and low priority items that can be addressed over a longer period of time.

It is not only possible for assistant principals to spend all their work time managing daily operations—such as testing; facility issues; student discipline; principal requests; district, state, and federal reports; faculty requests for everything from the broken copy machine to the lack of coffee in the faculty lounge; and so forth—it is also possible for assistant principals to feel that this is the way they must spend all their time. This issue of time spent, managing the daily operational responsibilities not associated with teaching and learning or with instructional leadership, is one of the biggest challenges facing today's assistant principal.

Another challenge faced by today's assistant principal is the expectation for immediate resolution and feedback coming not just from external stakeholders such as parents or community leaders but also from internal stakeholders served by the assistant principal: the principal and the faculty. Teachers, like the principal, may find themselves expecting the assistant principal to handle mundane daily operations so that they have time to teach. Teacher union representatives may complain that there is too much paperwork assigned to teachers, there are too many regulations, and there is too much bureaucracy. Isn't managing all these noninstructional aspects of the school operation what the assistant principal is for? Teachers often feel they don't need another instructional leader in the school; they need a secretary. The assistant principal often ends up caught in the middle between the faculty's expectation of having their operational tasks managed so they can do their jobs and the need for the assistant principal to take the time necessary to provide instructional leadership support to those same teachers.

It is not just the faculty who may see the primary role of the assistant principal as manager of daily operations. Many principals also have this same expectation. The principal sees the assistant principal's main function as the management of specific and numerous daily operation. Building an instructional leadership team with the principal and establishing a set of expectations for both the organizational management of the school and the instructional leadership of the school are critical components for any assistant principal who wishes to be an instructional leader, as discussed earlier in chapters 1 and 3.

An additional complication regarding the increasing allocation of time for management tasks and the decreasing allocation of time for instructional leadership tasks is that this issue is not unique to the role of the assistant principal. Just as teachers and principals may delegate tasks to the assistant principal that result in the assistant principal becoming desk bound or consumed with routine management job functions, other stakeholders may delegate different management tasks to the faculty and the principal themselves. All of the adults in the building are in the same boat, under the same pressure to organize their time so that both the management of routine operational tasks that come with twenty-first-century education and the accomplishment of their primary mission—teaching, learning, and student achievement—occur with fidelity. Just think about the number of forms, requests for information, routine attendance reports, lunch counts, and PTA fundraiser documents the assistant principal or principal delegates to the faculty to complete. How many meetings, reports, memorandums, financial documents, assessment and accountability reports are being delegated to the school principal by district and state staff and policymakers? Parents and other stakeholders want the same instant feedback from the principal and the teacher as they want from the assistant principal. Teachers are expected to get all their grades entered into the system immediately so parents can see how their children are doing. The principal is expected to handle routine management tasks that did not exist in the past (for example, the myriad of new reports generated by policymakers wanting increased school accountability) or used to be handled by district- or school-based support staff (now downsized due to budget constraints). It doesn't take much for preparing to teach in new and innovative ways, improving pedagogy, or attending professional development workshops to become afterthoughts for teachers—activities that would be nice to do, if only time permitted. Too often, however, time does not permit. It doesn't take much for the principal to become an office bound crisis manager; responding to phone calls and emails; sitting in and directing meetings with stakeholders; and managing student, parent, and teacher issues of the day. Instructional leadership, collaborative team building, facilitating the primary mission of the school, effective teaching and learning become afterthoughts for principals—more activities that would be nice to do, time permitting. Just as with the classroom teacher, for the principal, too often, time does not permit.

The reality, however, is not that there is insufficient time; it is that there is insufficient time when teaching and learning tasks are not prioritized above routine management tasks. In other words, how the assistant principal, the faculty, or the principal prioritize time actually can result in a lack of time to accomplish the tasks necessary to achieve the primary mission of the school: teaching and learning. The following example illustrates this point. An assistant principal in charge of facilities at a large comprehensive high school is tasked with building the master schedule. Of course each class, each teacher, needs a room assignment. While building the housing plan, a seemingly intractable problem arises, and the assistant principal reports to the principal that there is a serious housing problem for the exceptional education teachers and students in the school. There are not enough instructional spaces in the school to house all of the exceptional student education (ESE) teachers and classes. There is an ESE housing problem in the school. The reality, however, is not that there is an ESE housing problem in the school; it is that there is an overall housing problem in the school that, as a result of the priorities and decisions made regarding the use of the space in the school, has become an ESE housing problem. The assistant principal could just as easily report to the principal that there was a ninth grade housing problem or a mathematics department housing problem. The problem became an ESE problem as a result of the prioritizing that took place regarding the use of the building. It was true that there was not enough space to hold all the classes. It was the prioritization of the ESE department as the last group to be housed, rather than the ninth grade or the mathematics department, that resulted in the particulars of the problem presented to the principal. Obviously some department is going to be added last to the housing schedule. Perhaps in this case, ESE is the appropriate department to prioritize this way. The department may be very small in size. The instructional pedagogy used by the department may accommodate a wide variety of physical spaces. The department may have volunteered to be flexible and accommodating regarding the facility shortfall. The administration may have a past practice of purposefully rotating who is assigned to nontraditional instructional spaces. What is important with all these explanations is not what the final priority list looked like but how the list was prioritized in the first place. Was the prioritization purposeful and based on a set of standards and goals, or was it random? Was the prioritization established collegially or in isolation? Just as there is a limited amount of classroom space in any building and housing all students will involve some prioritizing, there is also obviously a limited amount of time available for the assistant principal to accomplish this task. How the assistant principal prioritizes time becomes extremely important.

The very same issues surrounding the prioritization of the housing plan for the school can inform the processes used by the assistant principal, principal, or faculty to prioritize how time for instruction and related activities is spent in the school. When time spent on instructional leadership, on teaching and learning, does not appear to be sufficient or even occurring at all, it is usually because the activities surrounding instructional leadership have become a low priority for the faculty and the administration. Rather than a problem finding time for teaching and learning, the assistant principal could just as easily have a problem finding time for returning parent phone calls or completing the weekly student discipline report. The lack of sufficient time to accomplish all the tasks required of today's assistant principal is real. The lack of time to focus on instructional leadership, however, is the result of how that limited time is prioritized.

While a clean, safe, orderly, and well-managed school may be a prerequisite for instructional excellence, it is, in and of itself, not sufficient either for students to learn or teachers to teach (Chen, 2007). A clean, safe, and orderly school provides an opportunity for learning to occur but does not assure that learning is occurring. The more time the adults in the building are spending on routine organizational tasks, particularly during the academic part of the workday when students and teachers are at work, the less likely it will be that the adults and the students in the building are spending the time needed to reach their full potentials. Every effort should be made by the assistant principal to handle routine school management tasks when students and faculty are not on campus so that the assistant principal can maximize the opportunities for instructional leadership with teachers and students when they are in the building. When schools are organized, well run, *and* have all adults in the building focused as a team on the school's instructional objectives, the opportunity for effective teaching and learning goes up. Simply put, all high performing schools have adults in the building who are prioritizing significant amounts of time for the primary mission of the school: impacting the lives of children through instructional quality and student learning.

THE LEADERSHIP LOG

Here is a fundamental question every assistant principal should contemplate regarding the allocation and use of time. How much time does the assistant principal spend on instructional leadership? How much time does the assistant principal spend on necessary but routine management tasks? What percentage of the workday or workweek is spent on instructional leadership tasks, and what percentage is spent on organizational management tasks? When during the workweek is the assistant principal attending to routine management issues, when teachers and faculty are at work or before and after normal school hours? In order to answer these questions accurately, a few simple but necessary steps are required.

1. Commit to keeping an instructional leadership log.
2. Define those tasks that are considered to be instructional leadership or related tasks.
3. Define those tasks that are considered to be organizational management tasks. (See figures 9.1 and 9.2 for a list of suggested instructional leadership tasks and organizational management tasks.)
4. Review the instructional leadership task list with the principal and with faculty leaders to establish task validity.
5. Begin logging, on a daily basis for a minimum of fifteen workdays, the activities and tasks that actually occur. (See figure 9.3 for a sample time log.)
6. After three weeks of accurate and complete logging, calculate the percentage of time spent on organizational management tasks and

the amount of time spent on instructional leadership tasks. To be meaningful, the log must be valid. That is, the log must measure what was you set out to measured, what really happened from the moment the administrative day began to the moment the administrative day ended. In order to maintain this high degree of accuracy, you should keep the log with you at all times and fill it out as the day goes by, not at the end of the day. It is not effective to rely on one's memory at the end of a very busy day to list all the tasks undertaken during the day or the amount of time spent on each task. It is very easy for an assistant principal to be involved in hundreds of interactions with students, teachers, and stakeholders over the course of a typical workday. It takes discipline and practice to measure and log what type of work is actually occurring each day. Many events will occur that are not planned, that are not on the assistant principal's calendar or "to do" list. Unscheduled meetings, interactions, and issues will arise over the course of the day that are not reflected on any planning calendar.

7. If the leadership daily activity log does not accurately reflect the day's activities, that day's log should be discarded and begun anew the next day with a new leadership log. The goal for the assistant principal committed to becoming an instructional leader is not just to get fifteen days' worth of time logs; the goal is to get fifteen days of honest and accurate time logs. This is easier said than done; it is important, however, for every leader to know the reality of how the workday is actually spent. To know what needs to be prioritized, what needs to be done differently with the time allocated to the job, the instructional leader must know how the time allocated to the job is currently being spent.

THE 50 PERCENT RULE

The assistant principal who wants to be more than an effective school manager or part-time leader involved with teaching and learning and who strives to be a leader who impacts the lives of the students and teachers prioritizes time so that a minimum of 50 percent of the workday is dedicated to the primary mission of the school. The assistant principal who is an instructional leader understands the mission statement of the district and the school; has reviewed the goals and the objectives of the school improvement or action plan; and has reviewed the list of goals and objectives set forth by the school board, the superintendent, the principal, and the political and business leaders in the community. What every assistant principal will see, as a result of this kind of thorough examination of the primary mission of the organization, is that the list is dominated with curriculum, instruction, student achievement, and pro-

– Teacher Evaluations	– Hiring of Teachers
– Classroom Walkthroughs	– ESE/504 Meetings
– Parent –teacher Conferences	– Teacher Mentoring
– Staff Development Activities	– Community Involvement Activities (PTA, SAC)
– Monitor Student Performance	– Academic Data Analysis
– Lesson Plan Reviews	– Textbook/Instructional Material Selection
– Media Relations	– Professional Collaboration (PLC, Leadership meetings)
– Site Visits/Networking	– Curriculum, Instruction Committee Work
– Instructional Technology	– Self-Reflection/Assessment (Reflective Practitioner)
– Mission and Vision Building	– Research on best practices
– Grant writing	– Activities to support positive school climate
– Recognition of Exemplary Work	– Diversity Initiatives

Figure 9.1.   Instructional Leadership Activities

fessional development activities. It is a list of priorities that requires effective instructional leadership to accomplish. The high performing instructional leader recognizes that no matter how difficult to accomplish, the commitment to spend half of each workday on the primary mission of the school is not out of balance. It could be argued that spending just one-half of each day on these primary mission objectives is actually far too little. Why would leaders spend as much as half of their time on activities not directly related to the most important aspect and purpose of school?

And yet it has been the experience of this author that many school leaders rarely follow the 50 percent rule, including principals. Building time for instructional leadership into the daily schedule is a constant problem for all administrators. Many school leaders believe they spend the majority of the workday on issues directly related to curriculum, instruction, student assessment and professional development, but it is not until an audit of the actual workday occurs that principals and assistant principals can accurately assess how they spend time on the job. The need for school leaders to reprioritize the workday and focus at least half of that workday on the primary mission of the school, however, has never been more important. Today's school environment of high stakes student assessment, new instructional design systems, and new teacher evaluation systems relies on a comprehensive understanding of teaching and learning by the school administration.

In order to implement the 50 percent rule, the assistant principal and the principal need to understand the issues that prevent the implementation of the rule in the first place. There are five common reasons school leaders spend less than half of their time on instructional leadership. (See figure 9.4.) Several simple time management strategies can also be implemented to help prioritize leadership tasks. (See figure 9.6.)

Managing Student Discipline (*)	Student Safety
Facility Management	Textbook Management
Student Supervision	Student Tardiness and Absenteeism
Master Schedule (*)	Student Lockers, Parking, ID Management
Bus Assignments/Issues	Budget (*)
Report Writing)	Handbooks (Student and Faculty)
Coordinating Student Activities	Evaluate Clerical and Support Staff
Technology Management	Audits
Record Maintenance	Testing Plan

(*) Management Tasks with Instructional Leadership Impact

Figure 9.2.   Organizational Management Activities

1. Failure to Prioritize Instructional Leadership Tasks Ahead of Organizational Management Tasks

Time is a fixed resource. We cannot add even one second to a day. Time is also, however, a resource that can be prioritized. What instructional leaders do that managers don't do is assure that high priority tasks are done first and lower priority tasks are done later. A simple, but effective, approach to prioritizing the workday so that teaching and learning activities trump management activities not dealing with safety is to keep a daily "activity priority" list, with each item on the list categorized as A—high priority, B—medium priority, or C—low priority. (See figure 9.5.)

As an instructional leader, the "A" list should be dominated with teaching and learning activities. It is also helpful to keep a short-term, weekly and monthly "to do" list in addition to the daily list. Long-term objectives and activities needing to be accomplished that will occur over the course of the year should be a third type of activity list kept.

Just as task prioritization is needed to comply with the 50 percent rule, there is also a need to prioritize the hours in the workday. Begin by scheduling blocks of uninterrupted time for instructional leadership work that will be filled with the "A" priority list of instructional activities. A good way to start is to block off the first few hours of each day for "A" list activities. While there are routine management tasks often needed to get the day off to a smooth start, such as student supervision, placement of substitute teachers, or facility issues, the early morning and the first few hours of the instructional school day are a prime time to schedule instructional leadership activities. The typical day for an assistant principal is just going to get more hectic as the hours pass. Putting off leadership activities to the end of the day in order to handle all the management activities at the beginning of the day will often result in a failure to attending to leadership activities at all.

DATE: Monday, September 10

Activity Start Time	Activity Description	Duration	*Task Type
7:30	Email Review and Responses	20 min	"B"
7:50	Student issue in Cafeteria	15 min	"B"
8:05	Leadership Team Meeting	55 min	"A"
9:00	Bill- Weekend Plans	10 min	"C"
9:10	Grade 4 Walk Through	45 min	"A"
9:55	Leave for Test Managers Meeting	20 min	"C"
10:30	Test Managers Meeting	90 min	"B"
12:00	Travel Backs to School	20 min	"C"
12:20	Lunch Supervision	40 min	"B"
1:00	Schedule Clerical Evals	30 min	"B"
1:30	Teacher Observation – Bill	50 min	"A"
2:40	Bus Duty	30 min	"B"
3:10	Coffee and Visit Band Practice	15 min	"C"
3:30	Lesson Plan Review/Feedback	60 min	"A"
4:30	Return Phone Calls	60 min	"B"
5:30	Headed home (no evening supervision)		

"A" Instructional Leadership Tasks   **Time:** 210 minutes
"B" Management Tasks   **Time:** 285 minutes
"C" Other Tasks   **Time:** 65 minutes

Figure 9.3.   Sample Daily Time Log

A second strategy to assure dedicated time for instructional leadership activities is to build a weekly calendar that has a variety of dedicated time blocked out for 50 percent rule activities while at the same time having blocks of time for the routine job responsibilities that must be attended to. See figure 9.7 for a sample 50 percent rule weekly calendar. Just as the school administration would not casually cancel or rearrange the lunch schedule, except in cases of real emergencies, the assistant principal should not casually schedule management activities into instructional leadership time or have more than half of the activities on the weekly calendar supporting non-50-percent-rule objectives.

By committing the first few hours of each school day to instructional leadership activities on a regular basis, the assistant principal can maximize the likelihood that instructional leadership tasks will be high priority tasks. By identifying additional blocks of time in advance for the week and the month ahead dedicated for lower priority activities such as routine management tasks, the assistant principal can dedicate a minimum of 50 percent of the workweek to instructional leadership. (See figure 9.7.)

2. Failure to Take the Time to Make the Time

Prioritizing takes time. Today's assistant principal is busier than ever before. There are fewer administrators assigned to complete more tasks

1.) Failure to Prioritize Instructional Leadership Activities

2.) Failure to Take the Time to Make the Time

3.) Fear of Being Disconnected from the Office

4.) Fear of Weak Instructional Expertise

5.) Failure to Own the Schedule

Figure 9.4. Time Traps

than in the past. It is easy for the assistant principal or any school leader reacting to the day's events to say there simply isn't enough time to plan; the assistant principal is too busy during the day to plan for the day. For the reactive school leader, making lists of what needs to be done and prioritizing those lists on a daily, weekly, monthly, and annual basis are just too time consuming. Reactive school leaders will also say they know what needs to be done and don't need simple lists to remind them of the tasks at hand or how to prioritize those tasks. These leaders will also say that schools are too complex and dynamic, with too many moving parts, to anticipate what needs to be done on any given day or week. The reactive leader will say, "I never know what is going to walk through my office door, so how can I plan for it?" While every day in the life of a principal or assistant principal will include emails, phone calls, meetings, and other unscheduled events, these activities are not reasonable excuses for failing to plan. Failing to attend to the primary mission of the school because the events of the day were overwhelming is not an excuse the principal would accept from the faculty. A teacher would not excuse a student if the student said his work was not done because he was side-tracked by other assignments.

Just as planning daily lessons and weekly units of study is a prerequisite for instructional success in the classroom by teachers, high performing assistant principals should also recognize that careful planning at the administrative level is a prerequisite for effective instructional leadership in the school building. If assistant principals do not plan and allocate time for the high priority activities of the day, week, month, and year, they will spend more and more time putting out fires and less and less time serving the principal and the faculty as member of the instructional leadership team.

Impact: Instructional Leader Daily Activity Priority List

Date: Monday, September 10

Task   *Priority
-   AM/Lunch/PM Student Supervision   "B"
-   Complete Weekly Lesson Plan Reviews   "A"
-   Schedule Clerical Staff Evaluation Conferences   "C"
-   Schedule Meeting with Faculty Testing Committee   "B"
-   Attend Parent/Teacher Conference with Mr. Jones   "A"
-   Complete Locker ID Schedule   "B"
-   Instructional Walkthrough for Grade 4   "A"
-   Read Journal Article on Formative Assessment   "B"
-   Memo to Principal re Last Week's PTA Meeting   "B"
-   Create File for Mid-Year Discipline Report   "C"

- "A" High Priority – Instructional Leadership Tasks (Table 9.1), Student and Staff Safet

  Tasks, Time Sensitive Tasks Assigned by the Principal

- "B" Medium Priority –Time Sensitive Management Tasks, Midterm and Long Term

  Instructional Leadership Tasks

- "C" Low Priority – Non-Time Sensitive Management Tasks

Figure 9.5.   Sample Daily Activity Priority List

3. Fear of Being Disconnected from the Office and Out of Touch with the Events of the Day

Another common reason many assistant principals find themselves working primarily from the office rather than getting out into the school community, both within and outside of school, is the belief that the office is where the work presents itself and where the work gets done. With today's portable tablets and cell phones, however, school leaders are no longer disconnected from the office even when they are out working with students, faculty, and other stakeholders. The good news, and the bad news, for the twenty-first-century assistant principal is that the office comes with you twenty-four hours a day, seven days a week. The notion that the assistant principal needs to be office bound to handle a timely email or emergency phone call is no longer true. In fact, today's administrators face the opposite problem when trying to allocate a minimum of 50 percent of their time toward instructional leadership. The problem becomes not how one deals with office work when not in the office but rather how one stops dealing with office work when out of the office. How often do assistant principals and leaders at all levels of the organiza-

1.) Start Each Day With "A" List Instructional Activities

2.) Build a Weekly Calendar With "A" List Activities Scheduled

3.) Share the Calendar with the Principal

4.) Log Actual Time Spent on Instructional Leadership versus School Management

5.) Add the Time Needed for "A" List Activities if Warranted by the Time Log

6.) Don't Get Frustrated When the 50% Rule is Not Met

Figure 9.6. 50 Percent Rule Strategies

tion check their cell phones or tablets to see what messages have just arrived while in the middle of a meeting or conversation or classroom observation? What message are these leaders sending to the people they are working with regarding the importance of the topic at hand or the commitment to being an active and engaged listener if every buzz and beep from an electronic device is given a higher priority than the event at hand?

The high impact assistant principal gets out of the office and implements a simple yet effective set of protocols so that the 50 percent rule is truly in effect when they are out of the office and attending to the work of an instructional leader:

a. The effective assistant principal silences cell phones and tablets when engaged in teaching and learning activities with the faculty and student body. This may seem very disconcerting at first; there is a feeling of being disconnected from the world. After all, isn't every school leader supposed to be on call 24/7? However, the solution is simple.

b. The effective assistant principal establishes a system for receiving emergency messages with an assistant or colleague so that, on those rare occasions when an emergency arises, there is a way to be contacted. One way to do this is to have a specific individual in the organization, often a secretary or other support staff colleague, set up a unique "alert," a specific ringtone only to be used in the event of an emergency. When the assistant principal gets that alert, it is easy enough stop the activity currently underway and respond to the alert. It is important for all the stakeholders the assistant principal serves to know that it is only in the event of a time-sensitive emergency that the assistant principal will interrupt the work and, more importantly, the constituent's work to take a call or answer a text. When teachers, parents, students, or any stakeholders know

Impact: Instructional Leader Weekly Planning Calendar

Impact Goals: 50% "A" Instructional Leadership Activity

Week of: September 10

Date:

	Monday	Tuesday	Wednesday	Thursday	Friday
7:00					
7:30					
8:00					
8:30					
9:00					
9:30					
10:00					
10:30					
11:00					
11:30					
12:00					
12:30					
1:00					
1:30					
2:00					
2:30					
3:00					
3:30					
4:00					
4:30					
5:00					
5:30					

Figure 9.7.   Weekly 50 Percent Rule Calendar

that the assistant principal places a high value on the work they are mutually engaged in and only interrupts that work in the case of actual time sensitive emergencies, it is much more likely that all the stakeholders the assistant principal works with on a daily basis will feel valued.

c. Effective assistant principals share their calendars with their principals and assistants authorized to contact them in emergencies. With simple calendar-sharing software, it is easy to keep calendars current and the principal and appropriate staff informed about where the assistant principal is and what the assistant principal is doing.

The need to stay connected for instantaneous communication is not an obstacle to prioritizing time. No instructional leader needs to be office bound to be connected. Instructional leaders do, however, need to be engaged with all stakeholders and focused on instructional leadership tasks to be effective. While some of those tasks and some of that engagement can occur in the office, the majority of the work of the instructional leader takes place outside the office where teaching and learning is actually occurring.

4. A Lack of Comfort with the Knowledge, Skills, and Expertise Needed to Function Effectively as an Instructional Leader

Assistant principals often use position power to accomplish the routine but necessary tasks of managing the daily operations of the school. The power and authority to sign documents, order materials and supplies, approve routine facility usage requests, and a myriad of other administrative functions are easily learned and executed. These tasks are also easy to complete from the comfort and isolation of the office. The use of position power, however, is ineffective in communicating, motivating, and implementing a strategic plan that results in school personnel working as a community of learners focused on student success. To build and lead an effective, high performing school takes more than position power; it takes expert power. To help build and lead an effective, high performing school, an instructional leader has to be where the stakeholders are, and the stakeholders are not in the office. To help build and lead an effective, high performing school, the assistant principal, as an instructional leader, must have expert power in the areas of leadership, curriculum, instruction, student assessment , and professional development.

Often assistant principals, in addition to the many ad hoc job responsibilities that are routinely assigned by the principal or requested by the faculty, also have specific job responsibilities that are unique to that assistant principal's job description. The assistant principal may be in charge of student discipline, facilities, budget, or testing. While the assistant principal becomes proficient, and hopefully an expert, in managing these tasks, the assistant principal can become disconnected from the knowledge and experiences required to be proficient, to be an expert, in instructional leadership. A catch-22 can develop. The more the assistant principal is isolated from the experiences and activities needed to become an expert, with a valuable role to play in instruction, the less likely the assistant principal is to feel comfortable working on goals and projects that involve the very experiences and activities needed to acquire that expertise. To make matters worse, it is not only the assistant principal who ends up feeling less and less comfortable serving as an instructional leader; it is also the principal and the faculty who feel less comfortable.

This author has never seen an office bound or management task bound assistant principal spend a minimum of 50 percent of the workday on activities that would be considered leadership tasks, not management tasks. Office bound assistant principals are not considered instructional leaders by the faculty or the principal. This is because the office bound assistant principal cannot be an instructional leader. The good news, however, is that the reverse is also true. This author has never seen an assistant principal who was spending at least 50 percent of their day on leadership activities not considered by others as an instructional expert and a valuable member of the instructional leadership team of the school.

5. Failure to Take Ownership of, and Accountability for, the Schedule

A fifth reason that many assistant principals find themselves bound to the office, unable to allocate the time needed to be in classrooms and teacher meetings as an instructional leader, is the inability or unwillingness to control the calendar. Simply put, calendars are tools for scheduling when one is going to undertake certain activities. All school administrators knows exactly when lunch will be served each day. They know when the third period bell will ring and when the Monday afternoon faculty meeting will start and end. The effective manager of the school day is an expert at time control, at scheduling the day down to the minute, for students and teachers. Pick any time of day and ask an assistant principal what class period it is or where Mrs. Jones, the Algebra 1 teacher currently is, and he or she will be able to answer the question. It is ironic that these same administrators are often, at the same time, unable to schedule their own workdays. It is as if the calendar for the assistant principal belongs to the community at large and is a blank slate to be scheduled on a first come, first serve basis, to address whatever issues arise during the day, regardless of the priority of those issues or the priorities of the assistant principal. Since it is a near certainty that a myriad of issues will arise every day, the calendar will typically fill to capacity. The assistant principal will certainly have a busy day. It will fill to capacity, however, without regard to the primary goals and needs of the school, the principal, or the faculty. The only way that the calendar can open, hold, and sustain the time needed for the primary tasks associated with instructional leadership is for the owner of the calendar, in this case the assistant principal, to take control of the day by taking control of the calendar. If assistant principals can dedicate and maintain dedicated time for all the students g and teachers in the building to attend to teaching and learning, they can also dedicate time into the calendar for their own work on leading teaching and learning.

IV

The Assistant Principal and Daily Operations

TEN

Managing Student Conduct versus Leading Students

Whether the assignment is a small elementary school or a large, comprehensive high school, managing student conduct is a job responsibility most assistant principals will face. Teachers expect administrators to assume responsibility for handling behavioral issues when the teacher refers a student to the office. How the classroom teacher views the effectiveness with which the assistant principal responds to the inevitable student violation of the code of conduct is a key component of the overall perception the faculty will have of the assistant principal. Even if the assistant principal is excellent at other job functions, failure to effectively manage student discipline issues or teacher expectations regarding the management of student conduct can have a negative impact on the working relationship between the assistant principal and the faculty. How assistant principals interact with students not only impacts the overall job impressions from the faculty; it also has a profound effect on the attitude that students and, thus, parents, have about the assistant principal. When students or parents perceive the assistant principal as being unfair or inconsistent in the treatment of students, it can become very difficult for the assistant principal to build a trusting relationship with parents and students. When parents or students begin to consistently question the wisdom and fairness of the assistant principal's actions regarding student discipline, issues with the principal and district staff can also easily arise. Further challenging the issue of managing student conduct is the fact that all the stakeholders the assistant principal deals with on a regular basis — faculty, students, parents, and the principal — have preconceived ideas about what it means to manage student conduct effectively.

As discussed in earlier chapters, for the adults in the building to focus on instructional excellence, the school must have a strong management

107

foundation. An effectively managed school is a prerequisite for school effectiveness so that the faculty and students can maintain their focus on teaching and learning. A well-managed school is not necessarily an excellent school, but all excellent schools are well managed. The same management prerequisites occur in the areas of student safety and conduct. Students cannot learn and teachers cannot teach if the learning environment is not emotionally and physically safe (Brackett, Reyes, Rivers, Elbertson, & Salovey, 2011). Parents cannot, and should not, feel comfortable with their children's school if that school has a reputation as being unsafe.

While the management of student discipline is often viewed as a routine and often unpleasant part of the job, there is nothing routine or inconsequential about school safety or the management of student conduct. Failure to manage student conduct with skill and expertise will result in poor relationships between the assistant principal and every important stakeholder in the school: the teachers, the students, and the parents. Failure to manage student conduct with skill and expertise will result in a weakened school foundation, the foundation of safety that is a prerequisite for teaching and learning to occur. A safe and orderly school is not necessarily an excellent school, but all excellent schools are safe and orderly. School safety is the one issue that the principal, assistant principal, and every school stakeholder assign the highest priority to. The key to being effective as the assistant principal working with student conduct is to view the job assignment not as a management assignment but as a teaching assignment.

MOVE FROM AN INFORMAL CURRICULUM ON VALUES TO A FORMAL CURRICULUM ON VALUES

School is a place where children go to learn—a simple statement. This is a statement that the vast majority of Americans would agree with. The more difficult question inherent in that statement, however, involves what curriculum it is that students are sent to school to learn. Should what is learned in school be limited to the basics of reading, writing, science, and arithmetic? If so, which science, which reading, which mathematics should be taught? Should what is learned in school be limited to what can be measured on a standardized test? Is there a place in school for teaching values or appropriate behavior? If so, which values and which behaviors? This author believes the answer to these questions will remain contentious and consensus will remain elusive (Banks, 1993; Askey, 1999; Osborne, Collins, Ratcliffe, Millar, & Duschl, 2003; Loveless, 2004; Gardner, 2011). Entire educational philosophies from Dewey's progressivism to Hutchins's perrenialism to Hirsch's essentialism have been designed to answer the question, what is worth teaching and learning?

The debate regarding the appropriate academic content to be taught in school will no doubt continue.

What is not debated, however, is the notion that there are academic content and cultural values worth knowing, and the schoolhouse is the nation's largest current home for delivering that knowledge from one generation to the next. There is a consensus across ideologies that there is academic content students can and must learn in order to be considered educated. It is agreed that school is at least one of the significant places in which this academic content can be learned.

What about behavioral content, however? Is school a place where a curriculum of values, of managing conflict, of learning tolerance and respect for others can be taught? Can behaviors be learned, and is it appropriate to teach certain behaviors and skills for managing human interaction in school? The answers to these questions should be obvious, and the fact that the answers to these questions are often not addressed in school curriculum in a proactive or organized way is one of the reasons so many students graduate without the communication and coping skills needed to resolve conflict or function as a citizen. So what is the answer to the question of whether school can be a place where values and conflict management are taught, of whether behavioral skills and coping strategies can be learned? The answer is, these are the wrong questions to be asking. The question to be asked is not whether values should be taught in school but who society wants teaching the values that are already being taught in school. The question is not whether behaviors and human interaction strategies can be learned in school but who society wants teaching the behaviors and strategies that are already being learned in school. Should educators default these critical components of human development to students' peer groups and social media? Should educators default on their responsibilities regarding this important subject and allow the random, informal curriculum provided on a daily basis by peers, who have no formal curriculum or approach to educating one another on the social foundations our society expects all citizens to possess? The answer is no.

The instructional leader in the school recognizes the need to formalize the teaching of appropriate student conduct just as the instructional leader expects the school to have a formalized curriculum and instructional plan for academic content. The high performing assistant principal responsible for student conduct issues leads by seeing student conduct not as a series of rule violations to be managed but as an important part of the school curriculum dedicated to teaching students how to resolve conflicts in ways that respect the cultural norms of the school, society, and the dignity of each person in the school. The high performing assistant principal works relentlessly to shift student conduct from a management function to a teaching and learning function by instituting practices and procedures designed to teach the values and human interaction strategies that the society as a whole expects from all citizens.

MOVE FROM MASS PRODUCTION TO MASS CUSTOMIZATION

Most schools mass-produce their disciplinary systems and consequences for disciplinary infractions in the school. Codes of student conduct that attempt to outline every rule and every consequence for a rule infraction are produced in an attempt to assure consistency and fairness in the disciplinary procedures of the school. This mass-producing of rules and consequences are based on the notion that having every rule and every consequence laid out in advance will allow for a rapid, efficient, and consistent application of the code. Mass-production techniques certainly have their advantages. For example, they are great for factories. When the organizational goal is to duplicate the greatest number of products as consistently and efficiently as possible, mass-production management techniques may be in order. It's true that today's typical school structure was designed during the industrial age and the rise of the factory, and our school grade levels and grading periods resemble assembly lines, with each teacher working at their appropriate station on the line. However, human beings are not widgets, and the goal should not be to duplicate over and over the same response to any particular infraction of the code of student conduct but rather to educate each student as a unique individual to the best of our capacity as educators.

Educators accept the concept of differentiated instruction as a best practice without question. When it comes to teaching students the academic content and skill sets we want educated graduates to possess, we accept that one size does not fit all, that different learning styles, different academic readiness, different interests, and different talents make up the student body. We accept that the adults in the building also do not respond identically to any one leadership style or approach to problem solving. Effective leaders are expected to adapt strategies to align with the needs of individual schools and teachers. Why, then, would it be a best practice to teach students how to behave as responsible citizens and how to manage conflict effectively with a mass-production approach to student conduct? Just as the best teachers see each student as an individual and work to differentiate their instruction accordingly, just as the best instructional leaders see each teacher as an individual and work to adjust their leadership style accordingly, so too will assistant principals in charge of student conduct be most effective when they see each student conduct issue as a unique event with a unique set of facts and, most importantly, as a unique opportunity to teach the values and behaviors expected within the school culture and society at large. While seeing the management of student conduct as applying the appropriate punishment commensurate with the infraction committed may be efficient and consistent, it is not the most effective way to teach children why their behavior was inappropriate or what alternate strategies would be more effective in resolving the conflict or infraction in question. Learning to follow the rules in order to avoid punishment for breaking the rules teaches at the lowest level of ethics and morality (Kohlberg, 1971).

MOVE FROM CONSISTENCY AND TRANSPARENCY IN THE OUTCOME TO CONSISTENCY AND TRANSPARENCY IN THE PROCESS

A common paradigm among today's school leaders when it comes to student discipline is that consistency is critical. When every infraction is handled the same way, the assistant principal can easily claim that there is no favoritism in the school and that the consequences for all rule violations are clearly written and communicated to all in advance. How can consistency and fairness be maintained if there is inconsistency in the consequences assigned when rules are broken? While a mass-customization approach to managing student conduct may appear to remove consistency from the process or give the impression that consistent treatment or expectations of people aren't important, that is not the case. It is not that consistency doesn't matter; it does. When some rules are upheld and some rules are not, students may come to believe that some "laws" count and some only pretend to count. Students should never be treated differently because of their gender, race, or school status. It is crucial that students see the processes that the adults in the building take to assure fair and just treatment are consistent.

What the assistant principal in charge of student conduct should aspire to is not a consistency of outcomes but a consistency of process. Having every student who is tardy to class automatically assigned to a thirty-minute after-school detention may be a consistent application of the code, but it will inevitably an unfair and unreasonable application of the code. Not every set of facts around every tardy will be similar. The student late as a result of hanging out in the gym represents a different compliance with the tardy policy from the student late are a result of a family emergency.

What are the processes of managing student conduct that must have consistency and transparency? First, how school rules, expectations, and consequences are built must be done in a consistent and transparent way. Decisions regarding which stakeholders will be involved in the establishment of school rules and the consequences for breaking those rules must be made. Are the rules developed at the top of the organization and then given to the faculty and student body? Or is establishing a code of student conduct a learning opportunity for students to feel involved and responsible for a set of behaviors developed by the entire school community? Are systems in place to allow for parent and community input into the values and behavioral expectations the school will have for students? Are students given consistent and transparent input into the rule-making process and the consequences for failure to comply with the rules? Will faculty and students have a framework that is consistent and transparent for suggesting modifications to either the rules or the consequences? When systems are in place that define the school culture, the school climate, and the school expectations for behavior as part of a team process that includes all the key stakeholders and when these systems are implemented consistently, the opportunity arises to teach students how to collaborate with each other and manage conflict in a dignified and respectful manner.

Second, the due process rights for everyone involved in any incident must be consistently maintained. Whether an infraction impacts the right of the teacher to teach in a climate of dignity and respect or the right of a student to learn in a climate of physical and emotional safety, the need to have the administrator in charge apply, on a consistent and transparent basis, all the due process guidelines outlined in the school code must be adhered to consistently for every teacher and every student every time. The outcome reached, however, does not need to be consistent, and most likely should not be consistent, for every case. The process used does, however, need to be consistent for every case. The concept of moving from consistent outcomes to consistent processes is important if the assistant principal is going to lead students toward a code of ethics, as opposed to manage student violations of the code of ethics.

The assistant principal will face much greater dissatisfaction from stakeholders throughout the organization for failing to consistently follow the processes for managing student conduct than for failing to have identical outcomes for nonidentical events. A high performing assistant principal responsible for student conduct issues leads by seeing each student conduct issue as a unique event with its own set of circumstances and opportunities for solutions. A high performing assist principal sees the management of student conduct not as a mass-production event but as a mass-customization event.

MOVE FROM SCHOOL AS A MONARCHY RUN BY ADULTS TO SCHOOL AS A DEMOCRACY RUN BY ALL

For most of America's history, schools have functioned as autocratic institutions. The adults in the school were in charge, and the students literally had no rights. The notions that the "idle fool is whipt at school" or of "spare the rod and spoil the child" are deeply ingrained in American history and school culture (Greven, 1991). The concept that children should have access to the same constitutional rights as adults is fairly new to education. It wasn't until the 1972 case *Tinker v. DesMoines* that the Supreme Court ruled, "Student rights do not stop at the schoolhouse gate" (Rappaport, 1993). During the Colonial era and well beyond, common punishments for failure to comply with the school discipline code, such as stockades, today would be considered criminal child abuse. Thankfully, the nation has come a long way in recognizing the substantive and procedural rights of students in school. While due process is now afforded to students involved in conduct issues, the common orientation between the student in the school as powerless and the adult in the school as powerful still remains fundamentally unchanged. For most administrators, when it comes to managing student conduct, it is position power, not expert power or charismatic power, that is used to resolve the issues at hand. Even the assistant principal who recognizes that position power is not effective, as discussed in chapter 4, in leading the adults in the building will often revert to the use of position power when it comes to leading the students.

It is not just the management of student conduct that has historically been built on an authoritarian, top-down organizational style, the content of the curriculum and the delivery of the instruction in school also have a long history of teachers as the holders of all the power—or in the case of curriculum, the holders of all the knowledge. The student is the passive receiver of all that knowledge. It wasn't until the work of education reformers such as Horace Mann and John Dewey that we began to see education as opportunities for schools to teach and model democratic processes and values. For Dewey and other progressive educators, the school should function as a democracy where students are actively engaged in their academic learning as well as in establishing and learning the values of citizenship, responsibility, tolerance, respect, hard work— the values that are seen as part of American culture (Scharf, 1977; Moss, 1998).

For too many school leaders, handling student conduct is a reactive, top-down, and management process rather than an opportunity to lead students toward learning how to manage their own behavior or learning new skills to manage conflict. For too many schools, the adults establish the rules for the school and the consequences for breaking the rules. The adults distribute a code of student conduct listing the rules and consequences. The adults—the classroom teacher and, when needed, the assistant principal or principal—are responsible for enforcing the rules. What are missing from this top-down approach to managing student conduct are the students themselves. What are missing from this reactive approach to student discipline are all the opportunities for the faculty and administration to be proactive with students and parents about the code of conduct before student violations occur. When more time is spent building and discussing with students the expectations the school has for how everyone in the building will treat each other, less time will be spent enforcing the consequences of breaking those expectations. When students are involved in building the rules and procedures, the culture of the school, student buy-in toward those rules, and acceptance of the consequences of breaking those rules will increase. When students have a voice in establishing the consequences for common violations and are part of the discussion regarding the nonnegotiable rules and procedures for major infractions and the legal and social rationale for the nonnegotiable aspects of the code of behavior, student buy-in will increase.

A high performing assistant principal responsible for student conduct issues leads by moving the school culture from an authoritarian approach to more of a democratic approach to managing student behavior. This does not mean the assistant principal relinquishes responsibility for a safe and orderly school environment. This does mean that the assistant principal involves the students in the discussions regarding what that safe and orderly environment should look like and why. The proactive assistant principal establishes student committees to discuss safety and conduct issues. The proactive assistant principal meets with students in the classroom, in the cafeteria, at extracurricular events, in short, where the students are, in order to engage in dialogue about the cultural and social expectations of the school and how those expectations are applicable to the adults and students in the school. When there is a clear violation of the code of conduct and the assistant principal has met all of the due process obligations and determined that a disciplinary consequence is in order, the effective assistant principal is able to implement the consequence in a way that maintains a climate of dignity and respect for the student. The effective assistant principal will praise outstanding behavior in public but will not punish inappropriate behavior in public. The effective assistant principal will maintain a relationship with the offending student that respects the student while still holding him or her responsible for his or her choices. The effective assistant principal will allow students to begin each new day at school as an opportunity to do the right thing today, even if they did the wrong thing yesterday. Just as high performing assistant principals do not carry chips on their shoulders regarding grievances against the faculty, the high performing assistant principal does not stereotype students, holding on to the idea that students' past behaviors are a predictor of their future behaviors.

MOVE FROM TEACHING STUDENT COMPLIANCE AS A WAY TO STAY OUT OF TROUBLE TO STUDENT COMPLIANCE AS A SYMBOL OF A PERSONAL CODE OF ETHICS

For most schools, the earliest lessons taught to students about behavior involve assigning punishments to inappropriate behaviors and rewards to appropriate behaviors. From the first day of school, students are taught a list of rules and that failure to comply with those rules will result in some type of punishment; it may be as simple as the name on the board or sitting out free play. The consequence may be as severe as suspension or expulsion. Whatever the consequence the message is clear: comply with the rules in order to stay out of trouble. For the student who follows the rules, there is also a consequence: a reward; perhaps it is a gold star on the board or the ability to be a line leader to free play. Whatever the reward, the lesson learned is also clear: comply with the rules in order to earn rewards.

This behaviorist approach to managing student conduct with its systems of rewards and consequences may be an effective way to begin the journey of educating students to live as productive citizens, but it should not be seen as the comprehensive approach that results in students who graduate from high school with the skills to manage conflict or display tolerance and empathy for others. In order for students to graduate with the kinds of values and social skills needed for a healthy democracy to function, teachers and leaders must be role models and part of the social structure that demonstrates the value of a personal code of behavior, an internal code of ethics followed when there is no reward to be earned and when there is no punishment to be avoided.

A high performing assistant principal responsible for student conduct issues leads by teaching students that the purpose for following a code of behavior is not to avoid getting in trouble or to earn a reward but to develop a consistent and internal code of ethics that the student will follow in all settings, public and private, because that code represents the values the student has developed as an educated citizen.

ELEVEN

Partnerships

All educators like to talk about the importance of family and community involvement in school. Family involvement is recognized as a key component in any high performing school and as a key contributor to the success of individual students (Hoover-Dempsey & Sander, 1995; Henderson & Mapp, 2002; Hill & Tyson, 2009). Teachers, principals, and assistant principals will often bemoan the lack of family involvement in the school and cite family apathy as a primary cause of student failure. Unfortunately, too many educators often also view the amount of family and community involvement in the school as something outside their control. They see this involvement as something like the weather; it either happens or it doesn't and is disconnected from any actions educators might take.

The good news about family and community involvement in education, however, is that it is very much impacted by the behaviors and attitudes of educators as well as the types of procedures and programs schools use to attract and maintain active family and community school partnerships. There are many examples of schools, serving serve every segment of our society, that are able to maintain significant, ongoing partnerships with students' families and with the community. Even schools with no history of active parent and community involvement can build a culture that supports active and ongoing community engagement. What do these schools have in common? What are the attributes and behaviors of the school leaders who have successfully engaged with families and their communities? These schools, and the leaders who serve them, build bridges that provide access for families and their communities to engage with them and provide access for school communities to engage in the local communities. These bridges are not one-way streets requiring the family or community members to come to the school but are two-way streets both into and out of the school. These schools, and the leaders who serve them, build systems that engage their local communities rather than simply holding events and inviting community members to attend. These schools, and the leaders who serve them, do not delegate community engagement to others or expect the systems in place or the maintain of those systems to always operate after normal school hours. Nor do they expect faculty and staff to volunteer for all community engagement on their own time. Bridges are built not by simply inviting families and external stakeholders to join the school community but by designing systems that actively engage the educators with the family members and the community members who have a vested interest in the success of those students. These bridges are built by designing systems that incorporate family and community involvement into the ongoing operational processes of the school. These bridges are built because the assistant principal and the school leadership team are responsible for building them.

INVITING ENGAGEMENT VERSUS BUILDING BRIDGES THAT REQUIRE ENGAGEMENT

One of the most common mistakes school leaders make when thinking about engaging families and community members with the school involves limiting where and when that engagement might take place. Because educators spend so much time at the school, there is a tendency to think that all engagement activities between the community and the school need to occur at the school. But sometimes the school is not the most effective location for ongoing and meaningful engagement. In many instances, families do not live close by. Many parents may not have had good experiences in school themselves. Many parents are used to only hearing from the school when there is a problem. For these families, school is not a welcoming place. The high performing assistant principal builds bridges to these families and neighborhoods. The high performing assistant principal recognizes that when families can't or won't come to the school, the school must go to the families. This author has seen many effective school community collaborations occur not at the school but in the community where families live and work. For example, collaboration can occur at local neighborhood centers, local churches, or other schools that are geographically closer to the community being served. Schools can hold community nights once a week at the local Boys and Girls Club. Schools can hold parent conferences and tutoring sessions at local churches. Schools can conduct summer and after-school enrichment and remediation activities at a neighboring school in the community. Working with church and community leaders to establish these offsite partnership opportunities also helps to build permanent relationships with the community as a whole, not just the families who have direct ties to the school.

It is not just where collaboration takes place that needs to be rethought; it is also when it takes place and what types of activities are offered that deserve further attention. Just because school is "in session" seven hours a day, five days a week, 180 days a year, this does not mean that meaningful family and community collaboration must fit into that narrow calendar. Collaboration can occur whenever educators and families get together, whether it is before school, after school, during school, or when school is not even in session. It is also a mistake for the assistant principal and school leadership team to think that all collaborative actives have to take place after normal working hours, which requires the teachers and administrators involved to volunteer their time. There are several workable strategies that can expand the time educators have available to collaborate with families and the community while still receiving some type of compensation and recognition that this is a core part of the educator's job, not something that is done after the fact, time, energy, and interest permitting.

For example, the assistant principal may want to explore using Title 1 and Title 2 funds to support family engagement by funding a small number of "permanent substitute teachers" to cover some class periods so that classroom teachers can spend time with family members and community members for extended conferences or other collaborative activities during the school day. It is important that the school leaders in charge of hiring substitute teachers use only the best substitutes for this work so that instructional momentum in the classroom is maintained. Many school administrators use these substitute openings as an effective way to hire and screen prospective faculty for permanent job assignments in the future. For the substitute teacher, this can also be a great opportunity to demonstrate teaching skills to the administrative team and to teacher colleagues in the department. Outstanding retired teachers who are interested in working just one or two days a week are another good source for this type of release time for faculty members.

It is not just substitute teachers, however, who can be used effectively to provide release time for teachers to work with families and the community. Assistant principals can also build substitute time into their schedules for this purpose, as can other teachers on assignment or with teachers who do not carry a full-time student caseload, such as guidance counselors or media specialists. Just covering for a core classroom teacher for one day a quarter (four times a year) will send a powerful message to the faculty and the community alike that the assistant principal and other support faculty value the opportunity for teachers to work directly with families during the regular school day. The assistant principal who subs for a teacher is also sending a clear signal to the faculty that their work is valued and well worth the time out of the assistant principal's schedule.

While not a solution for classroom teachers, another effective strategy the assistant principal may use to build community and family collaboration time into the regular school day is to flex the work schedule for support faculty and school administrators. Not every support person needs to report to work and leave work at the same time. By flexing the workday, even if just for certain weeks of the school year, the assistant principal can create extended hours for school officials and community members to work directly with school leaders while still keeping the school employees on a regular number of work hours. For example, if the school has more than one guidance counselor, select identified weeks in which one of the counselors will come into work two or three hours later than normal and then remain at school for the same time period afterschool hours to work with families and the community. The same can be done with flexing assistant principals, school deans, or teachers on assignment hours. This author has seen large high schools operating with faculty, staff, or administrators on the site from 6:00 AM to 9:00 PM without having a single school employee working more than their regularly scheduled number of hours per week.

Finally, for small schools with a limited number of personnel available, the use of flex time can be an effective strategy for compensating employees who are working extended hours in order to serve the needs of families and community members. The assistant principal may assign one week during each grading period in which teacher leaders and other school staff rotate covering evening hours or weekend events with families and the community. These educators are then compensated by receiving time off from work during nonstudent hours or workdays. A faculty of just thirty teachers, each giving seven to eight hours a year of flex time support for community involvement activities will generate 240 hours a year of service to families and the community and only cost one day a year for the school in flex time; just one release day from pre- or postplanning or a faculty duty day.

HOLDING FAMILY AND COMMUNITY EVENTS VERSUS BUILDING BRIDGES TO FAMILY AND COMMUNITY PARTNERSHIPS

School events that invite families and community members into the school are often wonderful activities. The school open house in the fall, the holiday concert in the winter, the spring carnival, and the PTA spaghetti dinner are all examples of school-sponsored events designed with good intentions to connect the school to the community at large. These invitational events are important and provide opportunities for the school to showcase the work of students to interested family and community members. Like administering a school versus leading a school, however, these events are not sufficient to engage the community as partners.

There are significant limitations to the typical school-community event. First, the activity is an event for the community rather than a partnership with the community. Second, these events are invitational by design and tend to engage only those family members and community leaders who are already engaged with the school in the first place. Third, these events tend to be "one and done" annual activities. These events, when well done, can become part of the tradition, the culture of the school, and can certainly be a highlight for teachers, students, and the community as a whole. However, these "family night" activities do not rise to the level of sustained and meaningful partnerships with families and the community.

Too often, school leaders and faculty build community programs and events without engaging families in the planning process. The effective assistant principal working on family partnerships begins by talking to parent leaders to see what their interests and needs are. The assistant principal should speak directly to as many family members and community leaders as possible to gauge community needs. School partnerships built by high performing school leaders based on parent input can result in very diverse and rich programs not typically associated with the neighborhood school such as GED programs, family walking clubs, and dance and aerobic classes. Another resource for building ongoing community partnerships available to assistant principals is the local college or university. By involving institutions of higher education in the mission of the school, the assistant principal can bring not only the resources, expertise, and energy of the university faculty to the school, but also the energy and skills of the local university students. Summer programs on the university campus; field studies to the university facilities such as science labs, theaters, core academic classrooms; and music, cultural, and athletic events are just a few examples of the valuable opportunities that are available to the local school by partnering with universities. Many university assets can also be delivered directly to the assistant principal's school as a result of these types of partnerships. College students are often looking to do volunteer and community service work. The local school is a great place to do that work. P–12 students of all ages can benefit from seeing and working with college students, who can serve as role models. If the local university has an education department, there will be professors who are looking to conduct valuable research in the school setting as well as place education majors into classrooms for pre-service experiences.

The high performing assistant principal can build opportunities into the school that result in sustained family involvement. For example, when looking at all of the committee work that needs to be done at the school, the assistant principal can work to add family and community members as permanent sitting members of all committees. Too often, parents are limited in their service opportunities to PTA fund-raising

Chapter 11

committees, extra-curricular sports and club committees, or committees mandated by the district or state to have a certain number of parents or community members. While these committees serve important functions and certainly should have significant family and community representation, there are a myriad of other school committees that could benefit from the presence of family and community members. Why not have families involved on the budget committee, the curriculum committee, the calendar committee, or the master schedule committee? In short, unless there are compelling reasons to keep families off of school committees, the faculty and school administration should encourage every committee to be represented by as many stakeholders as possible, including parents and students.

Another way to build long-term partnerships with families and community members is to work with the student body to develop sustained projects that impact and involve the community in a positive way. School and community partnerships to support Habitat for Humanity, local food banks, local hospital and nursing home initiatives, local Boys and Girls Club initiatives, pet shelter and animal support projects, projects that support veterans and their families—these are just a few examples of meaningful, real-world activities that add great value not only to the students themselves but also to the community. These activities are sustainable over time and, unlike special event activities, require ongoing collaboration between the school and the community.

DELEGATING COMMUNITY INVOLVEMENT TO OTHERS VERSUS BUILDING A BRIDGE OF LEADERSHIP ACCOUNTABILITY

Too often, assistant principals make the mistake of seeing family involvement as something that should be delegated and then monitored. It is often the case that assistant principals will recognize that communicating with family members is important and take responsibility for making sure the teachers in the school know they are expected to communicate with the family members of their students. The assistant principals may send out reminder memos or ask teachers to let them know how many family contacts have been made over the last grading period. The assistant principal who is serious about the importance of family communication may even make sure that all the phone numbers and addresses for each student are accurate so that the teacher doesn't have to waste time chasing down a parent. Nothing is more frustrating to a teacher than to be tasked with communicating with family members and then not given the infrastructure support and accurate records necessary to accomplish the task. It is not reasonable for the assistant principal to have the expectation that teachers will communicate with parents but then not provide the infrastructure and support system necessary for that communication to occur. When there is an issue involving a particular student, the assistant principal will remind the teacher that it is important to notify the student's guardian of the issue and may even volunteer to sit in on a parent-teacher conference if needed.

It is certainly true that in order to be a high performing teacher, communication with families and involvement within the community are essential (Warren, Hong, Rubin, & Uy, 2009). This communication is not something that can be effectively delegated by the teacher to someone else and should be monitored by the assistant principal. Delegating and monitoring, however, are not sufficient. Just as teachers should be actively engaged with families and the community, so too should school administrators.

To be truly effective as an assistant principal working in the area of family and community involvement, however, the work must be modeled by the assistant principal for all to see. The high performing assistant principal will not ask any teacher to do something that the assistant principal isn't already doing. Just as high performing teachers model the work they expect from their students, so too should the high performing assistant principal model family and community engagement for the faculty to see. If the assistant principal would like all teachers to make a positive phone call home to all parents at least once each grading period, then that assistant principal should be making positive phone calls home to parents each grading period. If the assistant principal wants to start a program in which volunteer teachers and support staff walk home with students once every six weeks, then that assistant principal should participate by walking home with a student once every six weeks. If the assistant principal expects the faculty to develop a series of family night activities, then the assistant principal should also develop school programs and processes that engage the community. Or, better yet, the assistant principal should chair the committee tasked with developing those faculty family night activities and be a leader and active participant in every event with the faculty. Once teachers see the ongoing commitment to the work by the assistant principal, the likelihood for their own buy-in will increase.

The high performing assistant principal communicates directly with families and interacts in an ongoing way with community stakeholders. The assistant principal cannot effectively delegate this communication with the community to teachers or support staff.

The impactful assistant principal builds and maintains an infrastructure that provides everyone with accurate contact information and time in the schedule for community contacts and activities to occur. Building family and community partnerships cannot be something that only occurs after hours without any compensation, recognition, or release time for the teachers in the school. Building faculty and community partnerships cannot be something that is expected of teachers alone. School administrators also need to set the tone by actively building and engaging in community partnerships as well.

IT'S ALL ABOUT RELATIONSHIPS

It is hard to overstate the significance of establishing personal relationships with stakeholders. Personalization matters; when schools build relationships with families and the community, schools can answer questions directly so that myths or misinformation do not spread. When personal relationships are established, parents feel they have an advocate and a support system in the school; they feel connected to the school and to the principal and the assistant principal (Adams & Christenson, 2000). Successful school leaders often build systems that result in direct contact with every family in the school. These leaders may write a personal letter to every family; these leaders may call every family to welcome them to the school; and these leaders may hold family meetings with every family in the school. This author has seen all three of these strategies at work, and with great success. While this level of personal commitment obviously takes a great deal of time, the school leaders who commit to building relationships at this individualized level report that, over the long haul, time is actually saved. The reduction of the time needed to correct rumors or resolve issues based on miscommunication or mistrust more than makes up for the hours expended at the beginning of the year to establish relationships.

The value of building personal relationships is not limited, however, to the relationship between the school and its students' families. Personal relationships also matter with the local business community and the larger local community. Strategies such as supporting local companies with partnership opportunities will pay great dividends for the school. Whenever possible, use the local bookstores rather than national chains for your school book fairs, use local photography shops for your yearbook photos, use local food retailers for your pizza nights, and use local businesses for your student certificates and plaques. All these local businesses are paying taxes. All of these local businesses are more likely to be supportive, by both word and action, if they are actually partners with the school. Simply put, local partnerships between the school and the business community are just good business for all concerned.

Finally, in addition to building relationships with families and the business community, build relationships with the community as a whole. An effective strategy for community partnerships is to use holidays like Veterans Day, Flag Day, or Martin Luther King Day, not just as days off but as opportunities to teach students about the true meaning behind these holidays and to impact the community as a whole. On Veterans Day, have students write letters to veterans thanking them for their service. Have students participate in Flag Day through flag displays and celebrations. Have students develop their own school-wide service projects and implement them around Martin Luther King Day activities. Have students write to and visit local nursing homes to read to the elderly or participate in art projects. All of these activities allow the community to benefit directly from the work being done by the teachers and the students in the school. All of these activities allow the community members to see, with their own eyes, the quality of the young people in the school and the commitment of the teachers. In addition, all of these activities provide authentic learning opportunities for students.

BUILDING SUSTAINABLE PARTNERSHIPS

The true sign of success for the assistant principal who is committed to, and has a passion for, building meaningful partnerships with the local community and the families being served by the school lies in building programs that are sustainable over time. This author has seen amazing principals and assistant principals implement programs that grow from small pilots, often a good way to start, to large programs with multiple partners and significant community buy-in: "walk your child to school" days that began with less than thirty students and expanded to more than three hundred students; and math and science nights that began with one teacher and ten students and expanded to monthly programs that involved teachers from every grade level and several hundred students and families. These programs began as small pilots supported by the vision of one or two educators and then blossomed into large, ongoing programs that became part of the school culture.

While these programs may often start because of the passion and commitment of one or two people, there are strategies that lead to program sustainability that the assistant principal needs to recognize. Too often, charismatic leaders are able to implement outstanding and successful programs only to have those programs vanish when that leaders move on to a new job. To be successful, the school leader needs to build a culture that is self-sustaining and does not rely on any one individual for its success.

First, as mentioned earlier in this chapter, sustainability is enhanced when the leader serves as a role model. Second, sustainability is enhanced when the leader is willing to be patient and start small. Programs may take time to develop and may need to go through several iterations before successfully matching the needs of the community. The assistant principal working on partnership sustainability doesn't stop the work because a particular program is slow to develop or fails altogether. The assistant principal knows that any set of programs may take years to reach fruition or may remain small in its impact but continues to keep an eye on the big picture: partnerships matter. Building a culture of family and community involvement doesn't happen overnight. Third, school leaders enhance sustainability when they are positive about the work and celebrate successes big and small. The assistant principal committed to building partnerships should work to assure more overall positive communication with parents and the community about students, faculty, overall school accomplishments, than negative communication. Too often, the only time the community hears about the school is when something negative has occurred. Too often, the only time a family member hears from the school is when there has been a discipline or academic problem with their child. The simple truth is that positive communication works. Sustainability is increased when teachers are celebrated for their work with parents and the community. The effective assistant principal should focus the credit and the recognition for partnership work on the faculty, on the students in the school, on the community partners, and on the parents themselves. These celebrations and recognitions do not have to be large or formal in nature. Students earning school pencils or school pins; parents receiving bumper stickers, a positive phone call from the school, a happy gram from the teacher; teachers being highlighted in the local PTA newsletter or on the local closed circuit TV broadcast; bulletin boards highlighting the partnership work of teachers—these are just a few examples of actual celebratory activities occurring in schools that help to build a school culture that can last. Finally, school leaders can enhance sustainability by hiring like-minded educators. Assistant principals can, and should, play a key role in the hiring process. In large schools, the assistant principal may be the lead administrator in the early stages of the interview and selection process. All schools develop cultures. Some schools develop cultures that tend to support academic excellence for all children. Unfortunately, some schools develop cultures that tolerate mediocrity or are isolationist from the communities they serve. All of these school cultures are impacted by the quality and temperament of the adults in the building. High performing assistant principals can help change the or build school by placing a high priority on the recruitment, identification, and retention of excellent educators who share a common passion for teaching and commitment to the well-being of all students. Success also breeds sustainability. When family members and the community are actively engaged with the school, they are happier. Student academic performances rise. Teachers receive more support from all of these stakeholders, which increases morale. All of this collaboration increases communication and understanding, which are a prerequisites for building trust (Hornby & Lafaele, 2011).

Building family and community partnerships is time-consuming work. It requires dedication that is sustained over time. Why should the assistant principal, often burdened with too much work to do and not enough time to do it, make community engagement a priority? Because community engagement implemented at the highest level pays off in the academic success of students. Because teachers and school administrators can no longer reach every child on their own; it does take a village. The high performing assistant principal recognizes that family and community involvement are needed, if every child is going to succeed and be valued. Because family and community engagement results in a great deal of pride in the community for the school and builds a great deal of support for the school from the community. The important question for every educator is not, why commit to this work? With all that is known about the impact on children in schools when the family and the community is deeply engaged, why would any educational leader not commit to this work?

TWELVE

Policies, Procedures, and the Law

School has always been a place where American values are taught. The value of building and sustaining a democratic form of government, the value of hard work and education, the value of honesty and justice are all part of the "other "curriculum that helps to socialize students toward a common set of values, regardless of religious or political orientation. This values curriculum is not the tested curriculum found on standardized assessments or the core subject curriculum found on a report card or a student's schedule; rather, this is the curriculum found from prekindergarten through high school graduation and reflected in what we celebrate in our schools and what behaviors we reward and punish. Of all the American values we teach and model, however, the most fundamental is the value of freedom itself. The freedom to speak one's mind, the freedom to choose one's faith, the freedom to one's privacy—these are just a few examples of a deeply rooted and constitutionally protected set of rights that every American citizen possesses. Our founding documents, such as the first ten amendments to our constitution and the Bill of Rights, focus almost exclusively on the freedoms that Americans should expect from their government.

While the freedoms outlined in the Bill of Rights are cherished and put forward to students as the cornerstone of our democratic form of government, these freedoms have not always been granted equally to all members of our society. Our history is full of examples of the struggles that minorities, women, the disabled, and many other members of the culture have endured. The rights of children, and the role of schools in relation to those rights, have also undergone many challenges and transformations over the generations. Over time, however, the freedoms all Americans enjoy have expanded, and this expansion has extended into P–12 public education as well.

The effective assistant principal must understand and protect these basic constitutional rights that all students and teachers enjoy. While each state constitution, set of state statutes, and education administrative codes will certainly have its own unique characteristics, there are fundamental, constitutionally protected freedoms all P–12 students and teachers enjoy. The courts have also afforded specific considerations to educators based on the special environment that is the school setting. In particular, the courts have ruled that schools in America have a special mission of great significance to the country. That mission is, of course, to provide all children with a quality education in a safe and orderly environment. The courts recognize that the liberties associated with freedom of speech, religion, and privacy, for example, may have some targeted limitations when a student or employee is engaged in school-related activities. These limitations center around assuring that the overarching mission of the school, teaching and learning, can occur.

For example, students in school still have freedom of speech, but that freedom is limited if it poses a threat to the primary obligation of the school—assuring student safety—or if it causes a disruption to the primary mission of the school—teaching and learning. During chemistry class, for example, a student does not have the right to begin a discussion about the pros and cons of government subsidies for health care, thus, disrupting the science lesson. It is also important to note that students are to be kept free from undue influence on matters not pertaining to the curriculum from the adults in the building. Whether it is a classroom teacher, principal, or assistant principal, the adults in the schoolhouse are functioning as agents of the state and should not impose their personal view on nonschool-related matters on the students. Students are considered to be particularly vulnerable to the influence of educators, who hold great power and influence over students lives in school. Complexity and nuances exist within the rights students and teachers have while in school. The educators and administrators in a school are obligated to protect those rights while also protecting the mission and safe operation of the school. However, there are fundamental and easily understood guidelines that will help every assistant principal operate in a manner that is consistent with the rulings of the federal courts. Specifically, this chapter provides an overview of those student and teacher rights as well as the responsibilities the assistant principal has in three basic areas: student rights, teacher rights, and employee contracts.

THE ASSISTANT PRINCIPAL AND STUDENT RIGHTS

During the early years of American public education, the legal doctrine of *in loco parentis*, the doctrine that school officials were able to act in place of the parent when the child was at school, defined the relationship be-

tween students and educators in school. It is very important to understand, however, that this doctrine of *in loco parentis* has not been upheld
by the federal courts for many years. It is a mistake in both an understanding of the law and the implied power of the assistant principal, or
any educator, to believe that when students are in school, school officials
have the same rights over the students as the student's parents. It has
been more than thirty years since the US Supreme Court ruled that the
concept of *in loco parentis* was at odds "with contemporary reality and the
teachings of this Court" (*New Jersey v. T.L.O.*, 1985). The federal courts
have ruled repeatedly and consistency that public school officials are not
stand-ins for parents. When in school, the teacher, principal, and assistant
principal are functioning not as parents but as representatives of the state
and are subject to the responsibilities and limitations of government in-
trusion into constitutionally protected rights of students.

While the courts have ruled that school officials are indeed representatives of the state, the courts have not ruled that school officials have the
same power or hold the same position as police officers or other law
enforcement personnel. The courts have ruled that there are special considerations, special mission characteristics, of public schools that limit
some rights of students while they are in school that would be granted to
those same students outside the school setting. In other words, the "constitutional rights of students in public school are not automatically coex-
tensive with the rights of adults in other settings" (*Bethel v. Fraser*, 1986).
Some rights that students have in a public forum outside of school would
not be protected during the school day or during school-sponsored activities. The example mentioned earlier about the student wishing to discuss
the pros and cons of government-subsidized health care during class
time is one such example of limiting the freedom of expression in the
school setting. On the other hand, when someone's cell phone goes missing during gym class, efficiency, as well as control of the environment,
might seem to call for simply searching all of the students who were in
the gym when the phone went missing, that approach would in fact be a
violation of the right to privacy that dates back more than two hundred
years.

REASONABLE SUSPICION VERSUS PROBABLE CAUSE

The right to privacy, to be safe from unreasonable searches and seizures,
is a founding principle in our Bill of Rights. Our founding fathers were
subjected to searches and property seizures without any warning or documented cause by the ruling British government, who saw great danger
to their authority in the actions of the so-called patriots of the day. The
Fourth Amendment was born out of the strong desire to protect
American citizens from similar treatment by their government. As dis-

cussed earlier, issues surrounding student privacy and student searches are commonly faced by assistant principals, who are often on the front lines of managing student conduct and school safety.

The 1985 Supreme Court case *New Jersey v. T.L.O* addressed several issues that help guide and inform the proper course of action for any school administrator faced with issues of student safety, possible violations of school codes of conduct, and searches of students or their property. First, the court ruled that public schools officials cannot conduct an unreasonable search of students and that the Fourth Amendment remains in effect on school campuses (G. Epley, personal communication, August 19, 2014). In short, students' expectations of privacy remain in effect when at school. The court did find, however, that schools do have a legitimate and important obligation to maintain an environment in which teaching and learning can occur without disruption. The court concluded that the "probable cause" expectation for law enforcement to engage in searches of person or property was too high a threshold for school officials who have the added burden of maintaining and securing the special mission of the school, teaching and learning, as well as the obligation to provide a safe environment for the children within the school. For school officials, a lower standard of "reasonable suspicion" would guide the decision-making process. The legality of a search by an assistant principal, or any school official, is based primarily on the reasonableness of the search in question.

What then constitutes "reasonableness" when it comes to the actions of the assistant principal? The court identified two variables for consideration. First, was the action of the school administrator justified at its inception? In other words, was there a reasonable suspicion regarding the particular student being searched prior to the search itself. Administrative hunches, the past behavior of the student in question, and physical evidence that could easily have an innocent explanation are not examples of reasonable suspicion and have been found by the courts to be violations of students' right to privacy. It is always best to have quantifiable or describable evidence that the search will reveal the specific violation, along with documented reasons for the search in the first place. Examples that might constitute reasonable suspicion would be statements from other reputable sources about the incident in question, security camera video footage, or other evidence that would lead to a rational conclusion that the individual being subjected to the search was indeed the violator in question. Another good rule of thumb for assistant principals faced with issues of student searches is this: the more invasive a search is, for example moving from the search of a book bag to the search of the individual person, the higher the standard for producing concrete and significant evidence will be. This higher standard extends to the need for the search in the first place, which must be reasonably perceived to be a real threat to student safety.

In those rare instances where a group search is being considered, the standard for reasonableness is extremely high. It is not enough to say, "I searched this group of students for a missing wallet, because I believe someone from this group probably stole the wallet." The idea that "I know one of you took it; I just don't know which one of you took it" cannot meet the standard of reasonable suspicion and specificity. The very nature of the group search indicates there was no specific evidence toward any one of the individuals being subjected to that search (G. Epley, personal communication, August 19, 2014). In all cases, the assistant principal should have all the evidence needed to justify the search of an individual before conducting a search, not as a result of the search itself. Group searches should be conducted only in extreme circumstances in which the primary obligation of maintaining student safety is in jeopardy, issues involving weapons for example, and then only when the principal has been consulted.

A QUESTION OF BALANCE

The challenge for the assistant principal when dealing with student rights versus administrative responsibilities for student safety and for maintaining a school climate in which teaching and learning can occur is the challenge of determining what actions may be sufficiently destructive to the educational mission of the school or the safety of the students. The same guidelines that would not allow a missing cell phone to rise to the level of a disruption or a mass search of the students in the gym would allow this action if the case instead involved a reasonable suspicion of a student with a gun in the gym. In order to maintain the appropriate balance between student rights and the obligations the assistant principal holds to maintain a safe school environment, and to maintain the schools' primary mission of educating students, the effective assistant principal must understand the special characteristics of the school setting that the courts have consistently maintained: the differences in responsibility and level of evidence for administrative action against a student, the difference between probable cause and reasonable suspicion, and the rights of students regarding freedom of speech.

VIEWPOINT DISCRIMINATION

Discriminating against someone's right to an opinion simply because his or her opinion is contrary to the majority viewpoint or is personally contrary to the views of the assistant principal or the adults in charge is a form of viewpoint discrimination. The courts have ruled against schools that allow student speech on some topics and disallow speech on other topics based solely on the views being expressed by that speech. This is particularly true when the students are espousing those views during noninstructional time or during officially sanctioned opportunities for students to gather for a specific noncurricular purpose and when those views pose no threat to the safety of the school or the student body. Often this issue of viewpoint discrimination occurs when school leaders allow certain groups to use school facilities after hours but not other groups. For example, the school might willingly rent its auditorium for after-hours use by a protestant minister but then be unwilling to rent the same facility under the same conditions to a Sunni imam. The school might sanction the use of a classroom after school for the Fellowship of Christian Athletes but refuse to allow a student-led gay-straight alliance club to meet. This type of viewpoint discrimination—of allowing one group to meet after school but not another based on the belief that some topics or points of view are offensive and are not supported by the majority of school stakeholders—has generally been seen by the courts as infringing on the First Amendment right to freedom of speech.

THE ASSISTANT PRINCIPAL AND TEACHER RIGHTS

Just as students' constitutional rights do not disappear on entering school but are subjected to limitations that would not be considered constitutional outside the school house, so are teachers' rights, as public employees with a special mission, when they are performing their job duties. The courts have consistently ruled that, while on the one hand public employment does not mean civil rights are lost or are unprotected, on the other hand the Constitution does not provide the freedom for teachers or other public employees, including principals and assistant principals, to simply conduct their jobs as they see fit. This balance between the protected rights of employees and the employee's obligations to the employer centers primarily on the employee's scope of work. If the behavior of the teacher, or employee, is clearly impeding the proper performance of the duties assigned or is interfering with the mission of the school or the safe and orderly operation of the school, the claims that employee might make to be engaging in constitutionally protected activities become tenuous at best (G. Epley, personal communication, August 19, 2014). For example, teachers do not have the right to teach only the content or curriculum they see fit to teach or use only the instructional materials they deem to be appropriate. Teachers do not have the right to use their classroom as a "bully pulpit" to espouse personal views or complaints not related to the job assigned. Teachers do not have the right to refuse to comply with job tasks and expectations that are clearly connected to the requirements of the work itself. Assistant principals should not feel powerless or without the responsibility and the authority to intervene when employee conduct is harmful to the safety of the school or students or impacts the ability for students to learn and teachers to teach in an efficient and orderly fashion.

It is just as important to remember, however, that assistant principals and all other school leaders do not have complete control of their employees. As with students, the rights of all public employees remain in effect while at work. Employee speech and other constitutionally protected activities remain in full effect when the employee is speaking as a private citizen or on a matter of general public concern. The fact that that speech or activity might be uncomfortable to the assistant principal or express a point of view that is counter to the position of school leaders is not relevant or grounds for attempting to limit the activity of the employee. When employees are not performing their assigned work, they have every right to gather and address issues of public interest, including issues specific to the work of being an educator or specific grievances about working conditions.

As a school leader, the high performing assistant principal recognizes that the rights of citizenship afforded to both students and teachers remain in effect while at school or on the job. The assistant principal also recognizes, however, that the special mission all educators have to teach students the adopted curriculum effectively, efficiently, and in a safe and orderly environment do place certain specific limitations on those rights.

THE ASSISTANT PRINCIPAL AND TEACHER CONTRACTS

Contracts aren't always efficient. The procedures and protocols listed in contract language often add a layer of record keeping or other bureaucratic requirements for the assistant principal and the teacher to follow. For example, it might be easier for the assistant principal and the teacher to ignore all the contractually required preconferences, observations, and postconferences for the teacher evaluation protocol and just bypass all those meetings and proceed directly to the final evaluation. This author has seen administrators skip every step in the teacher evaluation process and proceed to the final report when the teacher in question was an outstanding educator and everyone knew it. Both the teacher and the administrator would rationalize their behavior by asking themselves why they should go through all the trouble and take all the time that is needed to follow the contract when it is a foregone conclusion that the final result will be an outstanding evaluation. This is seen as particularly justified by the administrator when the teacher in question would also very much prefer to go directly to the summative conference and complete the evaluation. There are many problems with this approach, not the least of which is the shortcuts taken represent a clear violation of the contract the assistant principal is obligated to uphold.

Written contracts always supersede verbal agreements. The fact that both parties have agreed to act in violation of the contract is immaterial. The fact that no grievance has been filed about the contract violation is also immaterial. It is important to note that a grievance can be filed by any member of the bargaining unit or brought to the attention of the bargaining unit by any stakeholder inside or outside of the organization. A parent, a reporter, or a student, for example, could easily bring a contract violation to the attention of either the school or district administration or to the attention of the appropriate union representative. The fact that there was a mutually agreeable verbal understanding or even an email or memo outlining the agreement between the parties would not supersede the contract.

All employee contracts are in place for a reason. These contracts have been mutually negotiated and agreed to and need to be followed. There are very real opportunities for school administrators to submit input during the contract negotiation process, as well as provide input during the time period in which the contract is in force to colleagues who are responsible for preparing for the development of the next iteration of the contract. The high performing assistant principal can and should participate in the contract development process. The high performing assistant principal should also, however, make it a high priority to understand the contract, implement the contract, educate others about the requirements of the contract, and correct as soon as possible any inadvertent errors or omissions regarding the contract.

Whether the issue of concern addressed by the assistant principal deals with a contract, the behavior of a student, or the behavior of a teacher or any other employee, it is important for that assistant principal to have a fundamental understanding of school law and the rights and responsibilities contained therein. It is also critically important for every assistant principal to remember there is a support system of superiors and experts within the organization who specialize in issues surrounding school law as well as district and state policy. When there is any uncertainty about the proper course of action regarding issues surrounding student and staff rights, constitutionally protected speech and behavior, or employee contracts, the prudent assistant principal should consult with the principal and identified experts from the district office regarding the particular issue in hand. In short, when in doubt, check it out.

THIRTEEN

The Assistant Principal and School Levels

It is easy to typecast assistant principals by both level and job function. Some school districts are even reluctant to move assistant principals between levels based on the assumption that the skills needed to be successful as an elementary school assistant principal do not translate well to the skill set needed to be a secondary school assistant principal. For these districts, the elementary assistant principal can be perceived as "not ready" for secondary school leadership, perhaps viewed as too child oriented or based on a perceived need for a more subject-area-oriented school administrator. Conversely, the middle or high school assistant principal can be perceived as "not suited" for working with elementary school teachers or students, perhaps viewed in just the opposite fashion: too content oriented for the elementary school setting. This author has served as a school administrator at every level: elementary, middle, and high school and found that, while the ages of the students obviously change and conversations with students and teachers may have a different focus, the core mission of the school and the core leadership skills needed to be a successful assistant principal are fundamentally the same, regardless of the level of the school. While typecasting does continue in many districts, the good news is that the trend toward identifying, recruiting, and retaining school leaders continues to move toward the attributes of school leaders that are needed at every school level, as opposed to the concept of a different set of skills needed depending on the school level.

Perhaps a more realistic and serious issue complicating the movement of assistant principals between school level assignments can be the differences in pay many school systems have in place for assistant principals based on the school level or size. Does the movement of an assistant

137

principal from a high school to a middle school look or feel like a demo-
tion to the assistant principal? Does the movement of an elementary assistant principal to a middle school look or feel like a promotion? If this is
the case, because of perception or actual salary changes, many assistant
principals can become reluctant to work and learn school leadership at
different school levels. Some school districts recognize this problem and
work to minimize the unintended consequences of moving assistant principals to different school levels by holding salaries constant when the
change of a leadership assignment is at the request of the district. Some
districts place a special value on having assistant principals learn their
craft at more than one school level and value that experience as a positive
attribute should the assistant principal be interested in seeking a school
principal position in the future.

Even when school systems take a proactive approach to compensating
assistant principals based on performance rather than school assignment,
and even when assistant principals are self-motivated to serve at a variety of levels in order to gain greater knowledge and experience, typecasting by job role can easily occur. In larger schools that have more than one
assistant principal, it is easy for one assistant principal position to become primarily a management position (facilities, master schedule, student discipline, and the like) and one position to become primarily an
instructional leadership position (curriculum, instruction, assessment,
professional development, and so forth). In small schools, with just one
assistant principal, it is also easy for the principal to assume the job roles
connected with instructional leadership and assign the assistant principal
the job roles connected to school management functions.

Fortunately there are strategies readily available that can result in the
assistant principal as a manager becoming an assistant principal with
management responsibilities who is an instructional leader. These strategies have been discussed in detail in previous chapters. How the assistant
principal builds relationships with the principal (chapter 1), with the faculty (chapter 5), with the teacher's union (chapter 6); how the assistant
principal uses power (chapter 4); and how the assistant principal uses
time (chapter 9) all play important roles in accomplishing the assistant
principal's goal of becoming an impactful instructional leader regardless
of school level assignment or particular job assignment within the school.

School level assignments do, however, come with unique challenges
and opportunities for the assistant principal. Often these challenges and
opportunities are nothing more than two sides of the same coin. For
example, the challenges that come with being the only assistant principal
at an elementary school or a small secondary school also provide the
opportunities to learn and work in all areas of school administration and
leadership. Fortunately, the strategies and skills the effective assistant
principal needs to meet these challenges and opportunities are the same
at each level. When it comes to best practice in instructional leadership,

when it comes to being an impactful assistant principal, changes in school level, in school demographics, and in school principal characteristics will not change the leadership strategies discussed throughout this book or how they should be used. The strategies and behaviors that work for school leaders committed to teaching and learning for kindergarten students and teachers also work for twelfth grade students and teachers. The strategies that build trust, communication, commitment, and team work in the elementary school setting work in the secondary school setting. Strategies to involve families and the community in a meaningful way with the school should also remain the same regardless of school level.

THE ELEMENTARY ASSISTANT PRINCIPAL

Overview

It is in elementary school that most students learn what is required in terms of adult expectations for learning, how to succeed as a student, how to work in groups, and how to work independently. Elementary school is where the foundational skills of literacy and numeracy are acquired and a foundation for success as P–12 students is built. Elementary school is where children's self-confidence as learners and as people begins to take shape. Research shows a correlation between the academic success of students at the conclusion of their primary education, typically the end of third grade, and their later academic success in high school (Balfanz, Fox, Bridgeland, & McNaught, 2009). Students who are retained in elementary school or middle school are also at risk for later academic failure (Kennelly & Monrad, 2007). It is not an exaggeration to say that the academic health of the elementary student is critical to the overall likelihood that the student will graduate from high school with the skills, knowledge, and disposition necessary to be successful in life. School engagement, and conversely school disengagement, can be a long-term process that can begin to manifest itself early in a child's school experiences (Christle, Jolivette, & Nelson, 2007).

While elementary school is, and should be, child centered and nurturing for each and every student, the academic stakes for students in today's modern assessment-driven elementary school could not be higher. Despite calls to reduce or even eliminate high stakes standardized testing for students in the primary grades, the increase in standardized testing in America's schools continues (Kohn, 2000). The recent trends are toward more and more high stakes standardized tests for even the youngest of students, with extreme consequences for both educators and children when those standardized tests result in failure. However, it is still incumbent on all stakeholders to foster a love of learning in elementary school students, an ability to cope with and learn from failure, the ability to retain the inherent curiosity and creativity that every child possesses, and the ability to acquire literacies that are so crucial and fundamental to the mission of the modern elementary school. It is working in this high stakes environment and supporting these critical mission objectives that the high performing elementary assistant principal functions.

Challenges and Opportunities

First and foremost, the high performing elementary assistant principal must be a generalist. As the only assistant principal on the campus, the elementary assistant is expected to have full command of all areas of school operations: from the school plant to the master schedule, from student discipline to student assessment, from the activities of the PTA to the procedures for teacher evaluation. In addition, however, the elementary assistant principal must also have full command of all areas of curriculum and instruction, of teaching and learning. Whether it is kindergarten reading readiness or fifth grade science, the elementary assistant principal must know the proper pedagogy for instruction as well as the academic content to be delivered at each grade level. This degree of job scope can only be accomplished by developing expert power, as discussed in chapter 4. The work of the elementary principal can only be effective if trusting collaborative partnerships are made with teachers, as discussed in chapter 5. Finally, the variety of job requirements expected of the elementary assistant principal can only be accomplished if time is managed in a way so that instructional leadership is as least as important as management leadership as discussed in chapter 9.

It is also at the elementary level where family members and the community are most likely to engage with the school as partners. Elementary schools tend to be more proactive in developing opportunities for parents and family members to participate in school activities. In addition, parents are usually more comfortable with the academic content being covered in elementary schools and are, thus, more likely to engage (Izzo, Weissberg, Kasprow, & Fendrich, 1999). If that engagement is occurring, it is incumbent on the assistant principal to facilitate and support that engagement; if that engagement is not occurring in a meaningful way, as discussed in chapter 11, it is incumbent that the elementary assistant principal takes a proactive leadership role in developing and nurturing that engagement. The elementary assistant principal should play a significant role in developing and nurturing a high degree of family involvement in the school. If that involvement is positive and ongoing for elementary school families, they are much more likely to remain involved in their children's education throughout secondary school.

THE MIDDLE SCHOOL ASSISTANT PRINCIPAL

Overview

If the assistant principal is the leader in the middle of every school organization, working between the principal and the faculty, then the middle school assistant principal is the leader in the middle of the organization that also functions in the middle of the overall organizational K–12 structure, working between the elementary school and the high school. It may be a cliché, but many middle school educators suffer from an identity crisis. Ask elementary teachers what they teach, and they will usually say a certain grade level. Ask high school teachers what they teach, and they will usually name a specific subject area such as algebra or U.S. history. Ask middle school teachers what they teach, and they will usually be somewhere in the middle, with some teachers emphasizing grade levels (student centered) and some emphasizing subject areas (content centered). Elementary educators are often viewed as child centered. High school teachers are often viewed as subject centered. Middle school teachers are often viewed as transitional teachers, no longer providing the nurturing environment of the elementary school but instead tasked with preparing students for the rigor and departmentalization of high school. Middle schools often serve as the educational setting for structural transitions, moving the student from a relationship with one primary teacher to relationships with six or seven teachers on a daily basis, as well as for social and pedagogical transitions. These transitions not only impact the faculty in the school; they also impact the students in the school.

Middle school students find themselves no longer with one teacher for the majority of the day but with five or more teachers. Middle school students no longer find themselves with one level of academic expectations based on the grade level (i.e., fifth grade) but with differentiated courses and the beginning of student stratification based on perceived ability levels such as regular seventh grade math or honors seventh grade math. All of these transitions in school structure and tone are occurring while the middle school child copes with adolescence and the transition from childhood to adulthood. All of these transitions present the high performing middle school assistant principal with a unique set of challenges and opportunities.

THE MIDDLE SCHOOL ASSISTANT PRINCIPAL

Challenges and Opportunities

In addition to understanding the core constructs of educational leadership as discussed throughout this book, the high performing middle school assistant principal must also have a thorough understanding of the developmental needs of young adolescents. Working with young adolescents, the middle school assistant principal is leading students who are "undergoing a myriad of personal transformations and experiencing rapid cognitive, physical, and social-emotional changes" (R. Shankar-Brown, personal communication, August 10, 2014). Middle school students are often the most susceptible to peer pressure, unrealistic notions of body image, and a myriad of other peer and societal pressures that can often make learning academic content in school a very low priority. Coping skills, both academic and social, are often underdeveloped in middle school students. Issues surrounding bullying and the formation of powerful student cliques can make middle school one of the most difficult times in a student's P–12 academic career. Family members who were active in the elementary school setting may begin to distance themselves from direct involvement in middle school activities. It is here, in this climate, that the quality of the adults in the building matters more than ever. Managing student conduct and conflict as described in chapter 10 is always important, but perhaps more so in middle school, where a student's sense of right and wrong is particularly strong but still under development. Establishing meaningful relationships, not just with the faculty and the principal but also with the student body can be particularly powerful for the middle school students and particularly effective for assistant principals, who add the role of student mentor to the job description. For the assistant principal who wants to impact the lives of students: be a mentor and a role model.

The work of the assistant principal in the middle school also has unique challenges when working with and leading the school faculty. Successful middle schools must be both strong academic institutions and strong social development institutions. If students are going to be academically successful in high school, the prerequisite academic skills and content must be established in middle school. Too often, students arrive at their first year of high school already so far behind academically that their chances of graduating from high school on time and ready for college and a career are greatly reduced. To address this issue, the assistant principal should be a leader in supporting academic rigor and readiness as a key part of the middle school culture.

If students are going to remain in school and graduate from high school, the connection to school and the value of education must also be nurtured through the middle school years. This requires teachers who are both strong in the academic content of their respective fields and who have an understanding and interest in the development of the young adolescent, socially and emotionally. Too often the student, who was an actively engaged learner in elementary school, leaves middle school disconnected from the joy of learning that may have dominated their elementary school experiences. For these students, school is no longer meaningful or relevant. The belief that school can make a positive difference in their lives is wavering. To reduce this tendency for young adolescents to become disconnected from school, the middle school assistant principal should work with the faculty and all stakeholders (see chapter 11 on community involvement) to build a culture of support and belonging for all students in the school setting. The National Middle School Association has identified key characteristics for building a culture and community that supports the education of young adolescents, including "building a school environment that is inviting, safe, inclusive, and supportive of all," connecting every student to an adult advocate to "guide that student's academic and personal development," and establishing "comprehensive guidance and support services" for all students (National Middle School Association, 2010). All of these characteristics for successful, high performing middle schools require school leaders who are deeply engaged in supporting best practices for the education of young adolescents. The high performing middle school assistant principal strives to provide expert power and collaborative decision making opportunities when working with the faculty on all of these areas of student development: academic, physical, and social-emotional.

THE HIGH SCHOOL ASSISTANT PRINCIPAL

Overview

American high school students are dropping out of school at alarming rates, now reaching more than one million dropouts per year (Balfanz et al., 2009). High school student academic achievement is under attack by policymakers, with high school teachers and teacher unions viewed by many as being self-centered and unwilling to assume accountability for student performance, and more and more policymakers now call large comprehensive high schools unworkable monopolies. Many state legislators actively support legislation that provides parent choice through vouchers, through home schooling, through charter schools, and through online learning. Today's high school assistant principal is a leader in the country's largest public secondary education institution during a time of great stress and transition. Because of the size of many high schools, the high school assistant principal is also likely working with a team of other assistant principals, as opposed to serving as the only assistant principal in the school or one of a very small number of assistant principals. It is here, in the high school, that the assistant principal is most likely to be assigned a specific, narrow set of job responsibilities, often resulting in the assistant principal being isolated from leadership assignments associated with teaching and learning. The comprehensive nature of the modern high school, coupled with the stresses on the system from external stakeholders, the challenge of operating a school that engages all students, and the tendency for high school leadership teams to use bureaucratic organizational models all lead to challenges and opportunities that are unique to the leadership role of the high school assistant principal.

Challenges and Opportunities

Many of the general challenges faced by all assistant principals striving to be strong academic leaders, such as building strong professional relationships with the principal and the faculty, working effectively with the teachers union, finding time in the schedule to work on instructional leadership activities, and the like, are a daily part of the high school assistant principal's professional experience. There are additional challenges, however, that are unique to the assistant principal serving in the high school setting, particularly the following four challenges. First is the challenge associated with being typecast by job assignment into a narrow leadership role (i.e., the assistant principal for facilities, the assistant principal for discipline, or the assistant principal for curriculum). This typecasting can occur from both the principal and the faculty. The principal often uses a bureaucratic model to organize the administrative work of the school by creating unique and specific job roles for each assistant principal. The faculty wants to simplify communication and work with a simple and efficient organizational structure that clearly identifies who they should see regarding any particular issue. Several strategies for managing routine management assignments while still impacting the school in the areas of teaching and learning were covered in earlier chapters. It is important for the high school principal in particular to focus on and utilize these strategies. Too often, it is at the high school level where assistant principals end up as school managers and not school instructional leaders. Using the strategies discussed in this book, regardless of the specific job assignments from the principal or the need of the faculty to have routine management decisions handled by the assistant principal, the assistant principal can be an active instructional leader in the high school environment.

A second challenge for the high school assistant principal involves communication. As discussed in chapters 1, 4, and 7, effective communication is a prerequisite for effective leadership. It is inevitable that the larger the organization, the more complex and challenging effective communication becomes. In large comprehensive high schools, the number of faculty, students, school administrators, and other ancillary school support personnel can make consistent and transparent communication difficult. Having consistent communication and messaging from the entire administrative team can be difficult. Unlike an elementary school, which may consist of just the principal and one assistant principal who need to understand and deliver consistent messages to all school stakeholders, the high school administrative team may consist of four, five, or more administrators all needing to be on the same page. Building a principal–assistant principal leadership team that includes a plan for communication in a way that is consistent and effective is critical to the success of the organization.

Third, high school assistant principals work in an environment where many of the teachers are delivering academic content at a level well beyond the academic expertise of the assistant principal. While elementary assistant principals should be expected to have content expertise across the grade levels and disciplines, it is not reasonable for the high school assistant principal to have command of the content knowledge contained in much of the high school curriculum and, yet, that same assistant principal is expected to be a curriculum and instruction leader in the school. To accomplish the task of becoming a curriculum and instructional leader in this setting, the high performing high school assistant principal recognizes that instructional leadership is fundamentally about pedagogical expertise and not about content expertise. The high school French teacher does not expect every assistant principal to understand French verb tenses. The high school advanced placement calculus teacher does not expect every assist principal to understand differential equations. What these teachers do expect, however, is for every assistant principal to understand best practices in instruction, in assessment, and in student engagement. These teachers expect the assistant principal to facilitate professional development opportunities in their respective fields. These teachers expect each assistant principal to be a problem solver, a consistent and transparent communicator, a link between the teacher and the principal—in short, a leader.

Finally, and unfortunately, high schools traditionally have the least amount of parent and community involvement in the daily activities of teaching and learning in the school (Izzo, et al., 1999). With the exception of booster clubs supporting extracurricular activities, many families who were very engaged with their students' education in elementary school tend to drift away from that same level of involvement once their children reach high school. It may be no coincidence that the high school students themselves are testing their wings of independence for the first time and are often not interested in having their families involved with the school either. The challenges and opportunities for building family and community involvement in school that were discussed in chapter 11 can be particularly challenging for the high school assistant principal. Those challenges associated with family and community involvement should, however, be undertaken by the high school assistant principal who is working to serve as an instructional leader in the school.

High schools, with all their diversity and complexity provide a vast array of opportunities for true community engagement. In every discipline there are opportunities for service learning appropriate for high school aged students. Journalism classes can work on investigating issues of local concern. Science classes can work with local governments on ecology-related projects. History and government classes can work with local elected leaders to lobby for legislation that benefits the community. English classes can partner with local assisted living facilities to establish pen pal relationships with residents. Career and technical education classes can work with habitat for humanity to build homes, internship opportunities in health care, banking, and government can be established. In short, high school students should be out in the world, want to be out in the world, and will find school a much more meaningful experience if they are out in the world working with community partners. All of these opportunities for community engagement, and so many more, can be established and led by high school assistant principals interested in community partnerships. These partnerships can be established and run by any assistant principal, regardless of primary job responsibilities. The challenge of community engagement in the high school setting is, in fact, one of the easiest opportunities for the assistant principal to impact the high school experience for students in a positive and profound way.

FOURTEEN

Pursuing the Principalship

The clear focus of *Impact: How Assistant Principals Can Be High Performing Leaders* is to prepare the assistant principal for excellence as an instructional leader. Whether the focus is on establishing a high performing leadership team with the principal; building positive relationships with the faculty that have a focus on student achievement and faculty empowerment; strengthening the leadership skills necessary to be a true instructional leader, or learning how to manage and prioritize the obligation to manage the daily operations of the school that are so often assigned to the assistant principal while still securing the time, focus, and skill set to be an instructional leader, the position of assistant principal, when implemented with passion and expert power, can be both rewarding and impactful. Assistant principals make a difference. As discussed in chapter 1, in today's complex school environment, it takes a collaborative leadership team consisting of a high performing principal and high performing assistant principals to accomplish all that is expected for students and from the community at large. It is a fundamental belief of this author that the role of the assistant principal as a high performing leader is a prerequisite to the success of any high performing school.

It is certainly true, however, that for many assistant principals, a primary career goal is to be hired as a school principal, to lead the school. For these leaders, the role of assistant principal is viewed as a stepping stone to the role of principal. Not surprisingly, the best way to be recognized as someone who has the knowledge, skills, and values to be a high performing principal is to demonstrate excellent knowledge, skills, and values in the role of the assistant principal. Implementing the strategies discussed in *Impact* and avoiding the traps that have been outlined will lead to a high performing assistant principal. It is from that pool of high

performing assistant principals that superintendents and district staff select the individuals to become school principals.

Colwell and Potter (2013) identified nine specific strategies assistant
principals who aspire to become a principals should incorporate into
their work and their actions. These strategies, when combined with the
implementation of the recommendations described throughout this text,
will facilitate the assistant principal's promotion to the principalship. Figure 14.1 provides a list of these recommended strategies.

Most of the recommendations identified by Colwell and Potter (2013)
will occur naturally as a result of implementing the strategies discussed
throughout the text. Setting goals, both short term and long term, that
focus on the work itself certainly makes a difference in preparing the
assistant principal to be high performing on the job. When the assistant
principal's goals are not about career pathways but about making a difference in the lives of the faculty, student body, and greater school community, then career aspirations tend to take care of themselves. Getting
involved with colleagues through networking as well as developing new
and innovative ways to accomplish the mission and vision of the school
not only promotes excellence in the position of the assistant principal; it
also facilitates the potential to be recognized by others as a likely principal candidate.

In *Impact*, it is clear that the definition of a high performing assistant
principal is one who looks and functions like the principal. It should be
the primary goal of every assistant principal to not just understand the
principal's job but to be able to do the principal's job, to be an instructional leader. This ability to lead like the principal is much more than the
ability to step into the role of "acting principal" when the principal is off
campus. The ability to lead like the principal is most clearly manifested
when that impactful type of leadership occurs on a daily basis, with the
principal, with the faculty, and with the community. High performing
assistant principals lead from the position they are in, just like they will

1.) Set goals for yourself.
2.) Get involved.
3.) Develop an action plan.
4.) Share your career aspirations.
5.) Learn the principal's job.
6.) Stay positive.
7.) Learn what the principal knows.
8.) Be flexible.
9.) Keep a current resume and portfolio.

Figure 14.1.   Principal Preparation Strategies

lead from the position they are seeking, and as a result are seen by superiors as fully prepared to assume the role of school principal.

For those assistant principals with career aspirations toward the principalship, it is also important to share those aspirations with the principal and appropriate district personnel. Remember to let your superiors know of your short- and long-term goals. District leaders will often guide the assistant principal who is seeking a school principalship toward mentoring programs, internships, principal preparation programs, or specific graduate programs (Colwell & Potter, 2013).

When all is said and done, it has been this author's experience that the best predictor of future behavior by a school leader is an examination of that leader's past behavior. Principal search committees look at the past practice of those being interviewed. What were the actual behaviors, practices, accomplishments, and leadership styles that were displayed by the applicant in their work as an assistant principal? Is the applicant able to articulate a vision of collaborative leadership? Does the candidate display an expertise in the field and a desire to continue learning the profession? These are the questions superintendents and district leaders attempt to answer as part of the principal selection process. The answers to these questions can be easily seen in the work of impactful, high performing assistant principals. In short, for most principal searches, the selection committee is trying to identify the highest performing assistant principals. Superintendents know that the high performing principals currently on the job were also high performing assistant principals.

With many more assistant principal jobs available in any given system than there are principal jobs, it is the best of the best that typically rise to the top and are selected for principal leadership positions. While serving as a principal partner, faculty partner, and an instructional leader will prepare the assistant principal to serve with success and distinction as a principal, it is the work accomplished, the differences made for both faculty and students, as an assistant principal that lasts and matters. The best way to pursue and secure the job of school principal is to be excellent and impactful as an assistant principal who is an instructional leader.

Appendix: Professional Organizations

American Association of School Administrators (AASA)
1615 Duke Street, Alexandria, VA 22314
Phone: 703-528-0700 | Fax: 703-841-1543
info@aasa.org

American Educational Research Association (AERA)
1430 K Street, NW, Suite 1200, Washington, DC 20005
Phone: 202-238-32000 | Fax: 202-238-3250
www.aera.net

American Federation of Teachers (AFT) AFL-CIO
555 New Jersey Avenue, NW, Washington, DC 20001
Phone: 202-879-4400

Association for Middle Level Education (AMLE)
4151 Executive Parkway, Suite 300, Westerville, Ohio 43081
Phone: 614-895-4730 or 800-528-6672

Association for Supervision and Curriculum Development (ASCD)
1703 N. Beauregard Street, Alexandria, VA 22311-1714
1-800-933-2723, press 1 (US and Canada, toll-free)
1-703-578-9600, press 1 (DC local)
+ 1-703-578-9600, press 1 (elsewhere)
Fax: 703-575-5400

International Reading Association (IRA)
800 Barksdale Road, PO Box 8139, Newark, DE 19714-8139
Phone: 1-800-336-7323 (US and Canada), +302-731-1600 (elsewhere)
Fax: 302-731-1057
customerservice@reading.org

National Academy Foundation (NAF)
218 West 40th Street, 5th Floor, New York, NY 10018
Phone: 212-635-2400 | Fax: 212-635-2409

National Association of Elementary School Principals (NAESP)
1615 Duke Street, Alexandria, VA 22314

Phone: 800-386-2377 or 703-684-3345 | Fax: 800-396-2377 or 703-549-5568
Office hours: 8:30 a.m.–5:00 p.m. eastern time
naesp@naesp.org

National Association of Secondary School Principals (NASSP)
1904 Association Drive, Reston, VA 20191-1537
Phone: 703-860-0200 Front Desk, 800-253-7746 Membership
Fax: 703-476-5432 Front Desk, 703-860-3422 Membership

National Education Association (NEA)
1201 16th Street, NW, Washington, DC 20036-3290
Phone: 202-833-4000 | Fax: 202-822-7974
Monday–Friday 8:30 a.m.–4:30 p.m. eastern time

National Parent Teachers Association (PTA)
1250 N. Pitt Street Alexandria, Virginia 22314
Phone: 703-518-1200 or 800-307-4782 | Fax: 703-836-0942
info@pta.org

National Staff Development Council (NSDC) — Learning Forward
504 South Locust Street, Oxford, OH 45056
Phone: 800-727-7288 | Fax: 513-523-0638
office@learningforward.org

Bibliography

Adams, K. S., & Christenson, S. L. (2000). Trust and the family-school relationship examination of parent-teacher differences in elementary and secondary grades. *Journal of School Psychology, 38*(5), 477–497.

Aronson, J., Zimmerman, J., & Carlos, L. (1999). *Improving student achievement by extending school: Is it just a matter of time?* San Francisco, CA: WestEd.

Aschburner, S. (2011). *NBA's "average" salary—$5.15 M—a trendy, touchy subject.* Retrieved from http://www.nba.com/2011/news/features/steve_aschburner/08/19/average-salary/index.html

Ashkanasy, N. M., & Tse, B. (2000). Transformational leadership as management of emotion: A conceptual review. In N. M. Ashkanasy, C. E. Härtel, & W. J. Zerbe, (Eds.), *Emotions in the workplace: Research, theory, and practice* (221–235). Westport, CT: Quorum Books/Greenwood Publishing Group.

Askey, R. (1999). Knowing and teaching elementary mathematics. *American Educator, 23,* 6–13.

Avolio, B. J. (1999). *Full leadership development: Building the vital forces in organizations.* Thousand Oaks, CA: Sage.

Baldoni, J. (2004). Powerful leadership communication. *Leader to Leader, 2004*(32), 20–24.

Balfanz, R., Fox, J. H., Bridgeland, J. M., & McNaught, M. (2009). *Grad nation: A guidebook to help communities tackle the dropout crisis.* Washington, DC: America's Promise Alliance.

Banks, J. A. (1993). The canon debate, knowledge construction, and multicultural education. *Educational Researcher, 22*(5), 4–14.

Bates, R. J. (1980, March). *Bureaucracy, professionalism and knowledge: Structures of authority and structures of control.* Paper presented at the Annual Meeting of the National Conference of Professors of Educational Administration, Norfolk, VA.

Benne, K. D. (1948). Leaders are made, not born. *Childhood Education, 24*(5), 203–208.

Bess, J. L., & Goldman, P. (2001). Leadership ambiguity in universities and K–12 schools and the limits of contemporary leadership theory. *Leadership Quarterly, 12*(4), 419–450.

Béteille, T., Kalogrides, D., & Loeb, S. (2012). Stepping stones: Principal career paths and school outcomes. *Social Science Research, 41*(4), 904–919.

Bethel v. Fraser, 478 U.S. 675 (1986).

Bird, J. J., Wang, C., Watson, J. R., & Murray, L. (2009). Relationships among principal authentic leadership and teacher trust and engagement levels. *Journal of School Leadership, 19*(2), 153–171.

Blandford, S. (2000). *Managing professional development in schools.* London, UK: Routledge.

Blasé, J., & Blasé, J. (2000). Effective instructional leadership: Teachers' perspectives on how principals promote teaching and learning in schools. *Journal of Educational Administration, 38*(2), 130–141.

Blum, R. W. (2005). A case for school connectedness. *Educational Leadership, 62*(7), 16–20.

Bogler, R. (2001). The influence of leadership style on teacher job satisfaction. *Administration Quarterly, 37*(5), 662–683.

153

Brackett, M. A., Reyes, M. R., Rivers, S. E., Elbertson, N. A., & Salovey, P. (2011). Classroom emotional climate, teacher affiliation, and student conduct. *Journal of Classroom Interaction, 46*(1), 27–36.

Brown, J., & Munn, P. (2008). School violence as a social problem: Charting the rise of the problem and the emerging specialist field. *International Studies in Sociology of Education, 18*(3–4), 219–230.

Brunetti, G. J. (2001). Why do they teach? A study of job satisfaction among long-term highschool teachers. *Teacher Education Quarterly, 28*(3), 49–74.

Burke, C. S., Sims, D. E., Lazzara, E. H., & Salas, E. (2007). Trust in leadership: A multi-level review and integration. *Leadership Quarterly, 18*(6), 606–632.

Burns, J. M. (1978). *Leadership.* New York: Harper and Row.

Caprara, G. V., Barbaranelli, C., Steca, P., & Malone, P. S. (2006). Teachers' self-efficacy beliefs as determinants of job satisfaction and students' academic achievement: A study at the school level. *Journal of School Psychology, 44*(6), 473–490.

Cerit, Y. (2009). The effects of servant leadership behaviors of school principals on teachers' job satisfaction. *Educational Management Administration & Leadership, 37*(5), 600–623.

Chen, G. (2007). School disorder and student achievement: A study of New York City elementary schools. *Journal of School Violence, 6*(1), 27–43.

Chen, G., & Weikart, L. A. (2008). Student background, school climate, school disorder, and student achievement: An empirical study of New York City's middle schools. *Journal of School Violence, 7*(4), 3–20.

Chip on shoulder. (n.d.). Retrieved September 17, 2014, from dictionary.com: dictionary.reference.com/browse/chip+on+one's+shoulder

Christle, C. A., Jolivette, K., & Nelson, C. M. (2007). School characteristics related to high school dropout rates. *Remedial and Special Education, 28*(6), 325–339.

Colwell, C. & Potter, L. (2013). So you want to be the principal. *Principal Leadership, 14*(4), 48–50.

Conley, S., & Glasman, N. S. (2008). Fear, the school organization, and teacher evaluation. *Educational Policy, 22*(1), 63–85.

Cornell, D. G., & Mayer, M. J. (2010). Why do school order and safety matter? *Educational Researcher, 39*(1), 7–15.

Darling-Hammond, L., Amrein-Beardsley, A., Haertel, E., & Rothstein, J. (2012). Evaluating teacher evaluation. *Phi Delta Kappan, 93*(6), 8–15.

Darling-Hammond, L., & Richardson, N. (2009). Research review/teacher learning: What matters. *Educational Leadership, 66*(5), 46–53.

Davies, S. (2005). A revolution of expectations? Three key trends in the SAEP data. In R. Sweet & P. Anisef (Eds.), *Preparing for post-secondary education: New roles for governments and families* (149–165). Montreal, Canada: McGill-Queen's University Press.

Day, D. V., & Halpin, S. M. (2001). *Leadership development: A review of industry best practices.* Alexandria, VA: U.S. Army Research Institute for Behavioral and Social Sciences.

Dirks, K. T., & Ferrin, D. L. (2002). Trust in leadership: Meta-analytic findings and implications for research and practice. *Journal of Applied Psychology, 87*(4), 611–628.

Dobbie, W., & Fryer, R. Jr. (2011). *Getting beneath the veil of effective schools: Evidence from New York City.* National Bureau of Economic Research (NBER) Working Paper, No. 17632. Retrieved from http://www.nber.org/papers/w17632

Drath, W. H. (2001). *The deep blue sea: Rethinking the source of leadership.* San Francisco, CA: Jossey-Bass.

DuFour, Richard. (2002). Beyond instructional leadership: The learning-centered principal. *Educational Leadership, 59* (8), 12–15.

Education Commission of the States. (n.d.). *Leadership—District Superintendent.* Retrieved from http://www.ecs.org/html/issue.asp?issueID=285

Emerson, R. W. (1841). *Essays: First series.* Boston, MA: J. Munroe.

Farbman, D., & Kaplan, C. (2005). *Time for change: The promise of extended-time schools for promoting student achievement.* Boston, MA: Massachusetts 2020.

Fullan, M. (2010). The awesome power of the principal. *Principal, 89*(4), 10–15.

Fuller, E. J., & Young, M. D. (2009). *Tenure and retention of newly hired principals in Texas.* Austin: University Council for Educational Administration, Department of Educational Administration, University of Texas at Austin.

Gardner, H. (2011). *The unschooled mind: How children think and how schools should teach.* New York: Basic Books.

Gilley, A., Gilley, J. W., & McMillan, H. S. (2009). Organizational change: Motivation, communication, and leadership effectiveness. *Performance Improvement Quarterly, 21*(4), 75–94.

Goleman, D. (2000). Leadership that gets results. *Harvard Business Review, 78*(2), 78–93.

Goyette, K. A. (2008). College for some to college for all: Social background, occupational expectations, and educational expectations over time. *Social Science Research, 37*(2), 461–484.

Graham-Clay, S. (2005). Communicating with parents: Strategies for teachers. *School Community Journal, 16*(1), 117–129.

Gratz, D. B. (2000). High standards for whom? *Phi Delta Kappan, 81*(9), 681–687.

Green, R. L. (2013). *Practicing the art of leadership: A problem based approach to Implementing the ISLLC standards* (4th ed.). Boston, MA: Pearson.

Greven, P. J., Jr. (1991). *Spare the child: The religious roots of punishment and the psychological impact of physical abuse.* New York: Knopf.

Gruenert, S. (2005). Correlations of collaborative school cultures with student achievement. *NASSP Bulletin, 89*(645), 43–55.

Hallinger, P., & Heck, R. H. (2010). Leadership for learning: Does collaborative leadership make a difference in school improvement? *Educational Management Administration and Leadership, 38*(6), 654–678.

Hallinger P., & Walker, A. (2010). *Leading educational change: Reflections on the practice of instructional and transformational leadership.* Hong Kong: The Joseph Lau Luen Hung Charitable Trust Asia Pacific Centre for Leadership and Change, Hong Kong Institute of Education.

Hargreaves, A., & Fink, D. (2004). The seven principles of sustainable leadership. *Educational Leadership, 61*(7), 8–13.

Hargreaves, D. H. (2004). *Learning for life: The foundations for lifelong learning.* Bristol, UK: Policy Press.

Harris, A. (2002). Effective leadership in schools facing challenging contexts. *School Leadership and Management, 22*(1), 15–26.

Haynes, N. M., Emmons, C., & Ben-Avie, M. (1997). School climate as a factor in student adjustment and achievement. *Journal of Educational and Psychological Consultation, 8*(3), 321–329.

Henderson, A. T., & Mapp, K. L. (2002). *A new wave of evidence: The impact of school, family, and community connections on student achievement. Annual synthesis, 2002.* Austin, TX: National Center for Family and Community Connections with Schools.

Herzberg, F. I. (1966). *Work and the nature of man.* Cleveland, OH: World Publishing.

Hesselbein, F., & Shinseki, E. K. (2004). *Be, know, do: Leadership the Army way, adapted from the official Army Leadership Manual.* San Francisco, CA: Jossey-Bass.

Hill, N. E., & Torres, K. (2010). Negotiating the American dream: The paradox of aspirations and achievement among Latino students and engagement between their families and schools. *Journal of Social Issues, 66*(1), 95–112.

Hill, N. E., & Tyson, D. F. (2009). Parental involvement in middle school: A meta-analytic assessment of the strategies that promote achievement. *Developmental Psychology, 45*(3), 740–763.

Hoover-Dempsey, K., & Sandler, H. (1995). Parental involvement in children's education: Why does it make a difference? *Teachers College Record, 97*(2), 310–331.

Hornby, G., & Lafaele, R. (2011). Barriers to parental involvement in education: An explanatory model. *Educational Review, 63*(1), 37–52.

Hubbard, B. (2005). *Investing in leadership (Vol. 1): A grantmaker's framework for understanding nonprofit leadership development*. Washington, DC: Grantmakers for Effective Organizations.

Huffman, J. B., Hipp, K. A., Pankake, A. M., & Moller, G. (2001). Professional learning communities: Leadership, purposeful decision making, and job-embedded staff development. *Journal of School Leadership, 11*(5), 448–463.

Hursh, D. (2005). The growth of high-stakes testing in the USA: Accountability, markets and the decline in educational equality. *British Educational Research Journal, 31*(5), 605–622.

Izzo, C. V., Weissberg, R. P., Kasprow, W. J., & Fendrich, M. (1999). A longitudinal assessment of teacher perceptions of parent involvement in children's education and school performance. *American Journal of Community Psychology, 27*(6), 817–839.

Kennelly, L., & Monrad, M. (2007). *Approaches to dropout prevention: Heeding early warning signs with appropriate interventions*. Washington, DC: American Institutes for Research.

Kippenberger, T. (1997). Leaders are made not born. *Antidote, 2*(3), 10.

Kohlberg, L. (1971). *Stages of moral development as a basis for moral education*. Cambridge, MA: Center for Moral Education, Harvard University.

Kohn, A. (2000). *The case against standardized testing: Raising the scores, ruining the schools*. Portsmouth, NH: Heinemann.

Loveless, T. (Ed.). (2004). *The great curriculum debate: How should we teach reading and math?* Washington, DC: Brookings Institution Press.

McEwan, E. K. (2003). *Ten traits of highly effective principals: From good to great performance*. Thousand Oaks, CA: Corwin Press.

Merriam-Webster collegiate dictionary online (11th ed.). (2003). S.v. "charisma." Retrieved from Credo database.

Miller, A. (2009). *Principal turnover, student achievement and teacher retention*. (Unpublished manuscript). Princeton University, Princeton, NJ.

Moss. R. M. (1998). Book reviews [Review of the book *Education, society, and economic opportunity: A historical perspective of persistent issues* by M. A. Vinovskis]. *Community College Journal of Research and Practice, 22*(8), 761–763.

Mulford, B. (2003). School leaders: Changing roles and impact on teacher and school effectiveness. Education and Training Policy Division, Organisation for Economic Co-operation and Development (OECD). Retrieved from http://www.oecd.org/edu/school/2635399.pdf

Nahavandi, A. (2006). *The art and science of leadership* (4th ed.). Upper Saddle River, NJ: Pearson/Prentice Hall.

National Middle School Association. (2010). *This we believe: Keys to educating young adolescents*. Westerville, OH: Association for Middle Level Education.

New Jersey v. T.L.O., 469 U.S. 325 (1985).

Nguni, S., Sleegers, P., & Denessen, E. (2006). Transformational and transactional leadership effects on teachers' job satisfaction, organizational commitment and organizational citizenship behavior in primary schools: The Tanzanian case. *School Effectiveness and School Improvement, 17*(2), 145–177.

Osborne, J., Collins, S., Ratcliffe, M., Millar, R., & Duschl, R. (2003). What "ideas-about-science" should be taught in school science? A Delphi study of the expert community. *Journal of Research in Science Teaching, 40*(7), 692–720.

Peterson, K. (2004). Research on school teacher evaluation. *NASSP Bulletin, 88*(639), 60–79.

Pink, D. (2014, March). *Leadership and new principles of influence*. Presentation given at the Association for Supervision and Curriculum Development Conference, Los Angeles, CA.

Plihal, J. (1982, April). *Types of intrinsic rewards of teaching and their relation to teacher characteristics and variables in the work setting*. Paper presented at the annual meeting of the American Educational Research Association, New York.

Raelin, J. A. (2003). *Creating leadership organizations: How to bring out leadership in everyone.* San Francisco, CA: Berrett-Koehler.

Rappaport, D. (1993). *Tinker vs. Des Moines: Student Rights on Trial.* New York: HarperCollins.

Reynolds, J., Stewart, M., MacDonald, R., & Sischo, L. (2006). Have adolescents become too ambitious? High school seniors' educational and occupational plans, 1976 to 2000. *Social Problems, 53*(2), 186–206.

Reynolds, J. R., & Burge, S. W. (2008). Educational expectations and the rise in women's post-secondary attainments. *Social Science Research, 37*(2), 485–499.

Riggio, R. E., & Reichard, R. J. (2008). The emotional and social intelligences of effective leadership: An emotional and social skill approach. *Journal of Managerial Psychology, 23*(2), 169–185.

Robinson, T. (2010 May 24). *Sir Ken Robinson: Bring on the learning revolution!* [Video file]. Retrieved from http://www.youtube.com/watch?v=r9LelXa3U_I

Rost, J. C. (1998). Leadership and management. In G. R. Hickman, (Ed.), *Leading organizations: Perspectives for a new era* (97–114). Thousand Oaks, CA: Sage Publications.

Ruvolo, C. M., Peterson, S. A., & LeBoeuf, J. N. (2004). Leaders are made, not born: The critical role of a developmental framework to facilitate an organizational culture of development. *Consulting Psychology Journal: Practice and Research, 56*(1), 10–19.

Sawhill, I. V., & Morton, J. E. (2007). *Economic mobility: Is the American dream alive and well?* Economic Mobility Project. Philadelphia, PA: Pew Charitable Trusts.

Scharf, P. (1977). Moral development and democratic schooling. *Theory into Practice, 16*(2), 89–96.

Senge, P. M., Smith, B., Kruschwitz, N., Laur. J., & Schley, S. (2008). *The necessary revolution: How individuals and organizations are working together to create a sustainable world.* New York: Doubleday.

Sharkie, R. (2009). Trust in leadership is vital for employee performance. *Management Research News, 32*(5), 491–498.

Smith, C. (2014). *The NBA's Billionaire Owners.* Retrieved from http://www.forbes.com/sites/chrissmith/2014/01/22/the-nbas-billionaire-owners/

Snowden, D. J., & Boone, M. E. (2007). A leader's framework for decision making. *Harvard Business Review, 85*(11), 69–76.

Solley, B. A. (2007). On standardized testing: An ACEI position paper. *Childhood Education, 84*(1), 31–37.

Sprague, J., Walker, H., Golly, A., White, K., Myers, D., & Shannon, T. (2001). Translating research into effective practice: The effects of a universal staff and student intervention on key indicators of school safety and discipline. *Education and Treatment of Children, 24*(4), 495–512.

Stronge, J. H., Ward, T. J., Tucker, P. D., & Hindman, J. L. (2007). What is the relationship between teacher quality and student achievement? An exploratory study. *Journal of Personnel Evaluation in Education, 20*(3–4), 165–184.

Tschannen-Moran, M. (2014). *Trust matters: Leadership for successful schools.* San Francisco, CA: Jossey-Bass.

Tucker, P. D., & Stronge, J. H. (2005). *Linking teacher evaluation and student learning.* Alexandria, VA: Association for Supervision and Curriculum Development.

Warren, M., Hong, S., Rubin, C., & Uy, P. (2009). Beyond the bake sale: A community-based relational approach to parent engagement in schools. *Teachers College Record, 111*(9), 2209–2254.

Zepeda, S. J. (2013). *The principal as instructional leader: A handbook for supervisors* (2nd ed.). New York: Routledge.

About the Author

Dr. Chris Colwell is an associate professor and Chair of Teacher Education at Stetson University. Prior to his work at Stetson, Chris served as a classroom teacher, school guidance counselor, elementary, middle and high school principal, and as deputy superintendent for the Volusia County school board. Chris's school principal experience includes leading highly diverse elementary and high schools. As deputy superintendent, Chris led all federal, state, and local programs designed to support teaching and learning for Volusia County Schools.

In addition to numerous state committees and advisory boards, Chris served as president of the Florida Organization for Instructional Leaders. He was named Florida's Secondary Principal of the Year in 1997 and Volusia District Administrator of the Year in 2007. Chris is a frequent presenter at the state and national level on issues relating to education innovation and reform. Dr. Colwell's scholarly work centers on best practices in educational leadership at the school and district level.

89170959R00105

Made in the USA
Columbia, SC
10 February 2018